THE
PIANO OWNER'S
HOME COMPANION

THE
PIANO OWNER'S
HOME COMPANION

A REFERENCE GUIDE

BY

STEVEN R. SNYDER

SUNSTONE
PRESS

SANTA FE

Book and cover design by Vicki Ahl

Cover photograph by Carl Condit

Sunstone books may be purchased for educational, business, or sales promotional use.
For information please write: Special Markets Department, Sunstone Press,
P.O. Box 2321, Santa Fe, New Mexico 87504-2321.

Library of Congress Cataloging-in-Publication Data:

Snyder, Steven R.
    The piano owner's home companion : a reference guide / by Steven R. Snyder.
      p. cm.
    ISBN 0-86534-514-7 (softcover : alk. paper)
    1. Piano–Maintenance and repair. I. Title.

ML652.S7 2006
786.2'1928–dc22

                                                        2006019077

WWW.SUNSTONEPRESS.COM
SUNSTONE PRESS / POST OFFICE BOX 2321 / SANTA FE, NM 87504-2321 /USA
(505) 988-4418 / ORDERS ONLY (800) 243-5644 / FAX (505) 988-1025

CONTENTS

ILLUSTRATIONS

PREFACE

When you buy a car or major appliance, it comes with an owner's manual. Yet, for the last 150 years, piano purchasers have relied on myth and folklore passed down through generations for piano care and maintenance. Ideas such as cleaning ivory piano key tops with milk is one example of misinformation as "old wives tales." As a piano technician for the last thirty-five years, I have probably heard them all.

Today, we live in an age of information. This new and revised edition of *The Piano Owner's Manual,* originally published in 1981, gives you the facts. As in the original book, this new edition includes my response to the many new questions asked by piano owners. The questions keep coming, and so will my answers.

This book lifts the veil of mystery surrounding the expensive, impressively massive, yet surprisingly delicate piano sitting in the family room. It is an imposing piece of furniture, a visual masterpiece. Yet, first and foremost, it is an instrument. When played with skill, it produces beautiful music that can transport us to realms far from the room in which the instrument rests. Within the piano strings, plate, hammers, and case sleeps its magic. Hence, piano care and maintenance revolves around the piano's true value; its tone; its feel, its ability to respond to the pianist's desire. In the end, sound and artistry determine the instrument's worth.

Having a neglected piano sitting in your living room, unable to produce the music it was made for, is akin to having an expensive car rusting in your driveway unable to run. The broken car and piano are not being used for their designed purpose. To keep a car in shape and running it takes good working parts and proper timing. The same is true with pianos.

In the coming pages you will learn how tuning and timing, or in piano terms, *regulation,* keeps a piano in top operating condition. You will learn some basic piano terms and terminology used by piano technicians, so that you can understand the service person when they explain the piano's needs.

Essentially, this guide presents the piano as a simple instrument, with simple operating parts. It is the relationship between these parts, the timing, that creates the magic of piano sound.

In addition, you will learn how to help maintain your instrument by doing some of the service tasks usually done by piano technicians.

It is my hope that this new edition demystifies the piano, eliminates fear about the instrument, and makes beautiful piano sound accessible to all.

INTRODUCTION

As a piano tuner-technician for more than thirty-five years, I gained most of my experience servicing pianos in the customer's home. I worked for different piano companies in Boston, Los Angeles, and New York City. I tuned, regulated, voiced, and serviced pianos for recording studios, rehearsal studios, concert venues, accomplished concert pianists, and popular artists around the country. Wherever I went, I heard pianists ask the same questions and express similar concerns.

The Piano Owner's Manual is my response to my client's questions written in layman's terms. It is not a technician's handbook. There are plenty of technical piano books written by and for technicians. This work is designed specifically for piano owners. My extensive work in homes and studios gave me a special opportunity to talk with pianists of every skill level. From beginner to accomplished artist, most pianists want to know more about their piano, yet when they talk with a piano technician, they become lost in technical terms and esoteric concepts. Piano owners want to know how to clean a piano without damaging it, how to do common repairs, and they want an understanding of piano parts and function so that they can comprehend piano language when consulting with a technician about required maintenance and repairs. A concert artist needs a rudimentary understanding about piano function to gain the greatest range of expression from his instrument. The average piano owner wants to keep it in good shape to protect their investment. Both want similar information.

Through proper cleaning, moth protection, correct piano placement, climate control, and minor adjustments, one can eliminate costly repairs and enjoy thousands of hours of trouble-free music. A piano is one of the most esthetically beautiful, sensitive, yet durable instruments ever invented. When maintained properly, a piano can last over one hundred years. Pianos bring joy and fulfillment to millions of people. Hence, they are worth understanding and treasuring.

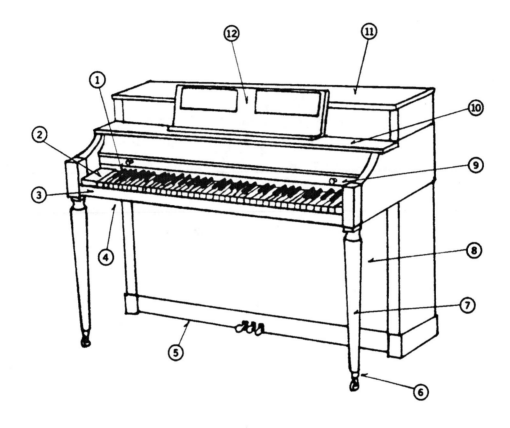

① FALL STRIP	⑤ BOTTOM BOARD	⑨ FALLBOARD
② KEYBLOCK	⑥ CASTER	⑩ MUSIC SHELF
③ KEYSLIP	⑦ LEG	⑪ LID
④ KEYBED	⑧ LOWER FRAME	⑫ MUSIC DESK

#1 Console Piano

1
PIANO TYPES

CONSOLE PIANO

A console piano is the most common vertical piano. A vertical piano is any piano with the strings in a vertical position, in contrast to a grand piano, which has strings in a horizontal position. Vertical pianos come in three sizes: *Spinet, console,* and *upright.* The size of a vertical piano is measured from the floor to the top of the lid.

The easiest way to identify a console piano is to measure it. The smallest vertical piano is known as the spinet, and measures about forty inches or less. The studio upright or console, as it is better known, ranges from forty inches to forty-nine inches tall. The largest of the three vertical pianos is the upright, which measures about fifty inches or more. (see illustration #3)

Another identifying feature of the console piano is the location of the piano action. A piano action is that part of the piano that transfers the striking force from the key to the string. As shown in illustration #6, the console piano action sits directly on top of the keys.

In the console piano illustration, the most commonly referred to cabinet parts are labeled. It is much easier to discuss replacements or repairs if you know the names of the parts, and knowing them also brings you a step closer to understanding your piano.

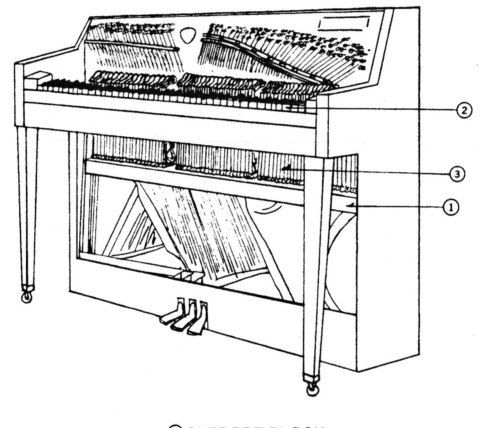

① SUPPORT BLOCK

② KEYS

③ DROP STICKERS

#2 Spinet Piano

SPINET PIANO

The spinet piano is the smallest of the vertical pianos. It has what is known as a drop action which means that the action is below the level of the keys. For a detailed view of a spinet piano action, see illustration #18.

In outward appearance, the spinet piano is much like the console piano because many spinets and consoles are similar in height. The major difference between the two pianos is the location of the action within the piano case. In the spinet piano illustration, the *music shelf, fallboard,* and *lower frame* have been removed to give a clear view of the drop action as it is placed in the piano.

The action is supported by a long block of wood (1) inside the piano. Since the piano action is below the keys (2), *drop stickers* or *lifter wires* (3) are used to attach the keys to the action. The spinet's drop stickers make spinet piano actions difficult for technicians to service because they can not reach in between the stickers to repair a faulty action part. When a repair is necessary, the technician must remove the entire action before attempting the repair. Removal of a spinet action can be complicated and often means higher repair costs to the spinet piano owner.

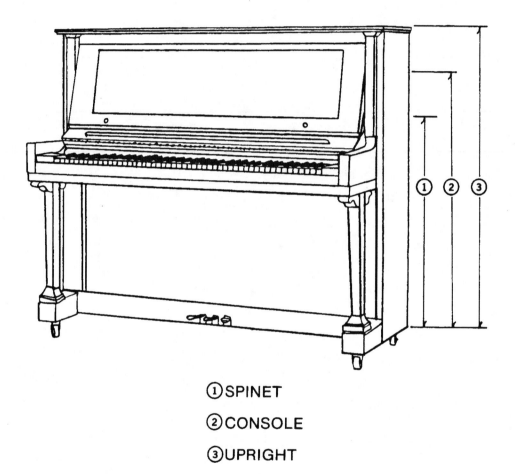

AVERAGE HEIGHTS OF VERTICAL PIANOS

① SPINET

② CONSOLE

③ UPRIGHT

#3 Modern Upright Piano

UPRIGHT PIANO

The tallest of the vertical pianos is the upright piano. Its added height gives it a richness and tonal quality comparable to a small grand. The illustration of a typical modern upright piano shows the difference in size among upright, console, and spinet pianos. All pianos are basically the same width, yet vary in length. The taller the piano, the longer the strings and the richer the tone.

The location of the action is the unique feature that distinguishes upright pianos from spinets and consoles. The upright piano action is located above the piano keys and rests on *stickers*. Stickers are usually made of wood and are connected to the action, rather than being attached to the keys as they are in spinet pianos. Stickers vary in length proportionally with the height of the piano. For a detailed illustration and location of a sticker, refer to illustration #7.

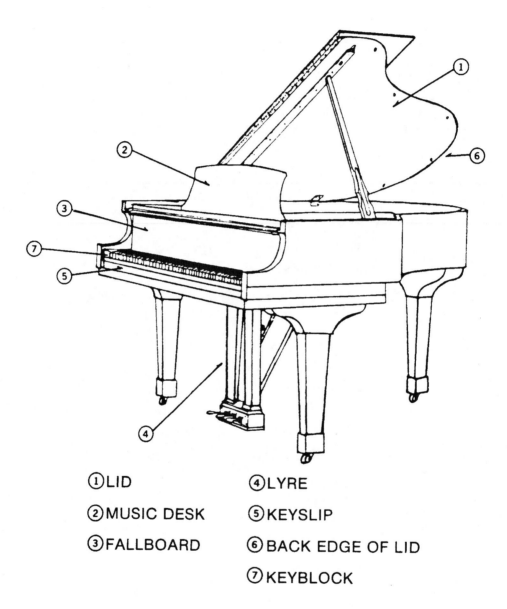

① LID   ④ LYRE

② MUSIC DESK   ⑤ KEYSLIP

③ FALLBOARD   ⑥ BACK EDGE OF LID

                    ⑦ KEYBLOCK

#4 Grand Piano

GRAND PIANO

A grand piano is a piano with its strings in a horizontal position. The most important feature of the grand piano cabinet is the length, measured horizontally from the *keyslip* (5) to the back edge of the *lid* (6). Grand pianos are built in progressive sizes from four feet eleven inches to over nine feet. Each size is about one inch longer than the next. Many of these piano sizes are given different names.

The smallest grand, usually about four feet eleven inches, is called the Apartment Grand. The Baby Grand measures five feet eight inches. The Living Room Grand is five feet ten inches long. The Professional Grand is six feet to six feet eight inches long and is the one most often used in recording studios. Pianos ranging from six feet eight inches to six feet ten inches are given the general name of Music Room Grand. The Semi Concert Grand measures seven feet four inches, and the Concert Grand measures eight feet eleven inches and longer. The added length given to Concert Grands increases the tonal quality, volume, and depth of expression needed to project throughout large concert halls.

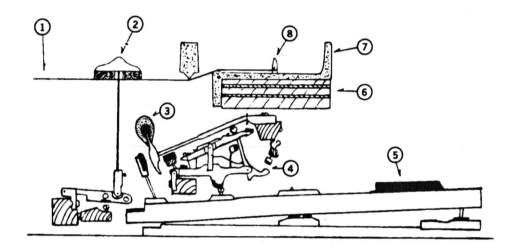

① STRING   ⑤ KEY

② DAMPER   ⑥ PINBLOCK

③ HAMMER   ⑦ PLATE

④ WIPPEN   ⑧ TUNING PIN
   ASSEMBLY

#5 Grand Piano Action

GRAND PIANO ACTION

The piano action, that part of the piano that transfers the striking force from the key to the string, is the heart of every piano. It looks complicated, but it is not as complex as it seems. My purpose here is to familiarize you with the basic parts of the grand action so you can identify these parts in your piano.

If you look at the Grand Piano Action illustration, you will see how a piano works. You strike the *key* (5) to play a note. The piano key is a solid piece of soft wood with the striking surface covered by plastic, or sometimes ivory. When the key is struck, it contacts the *wippen* assembly (4). The wippen makes the *hammer* (3) rise up to strike the *string* (1). While the key is depressed, the *damper* (2) is lifted off the string, and the note continues to ring until the key is released.

The parts shown in black (with the exception of the piano key) are felt. The hammer is also felt, glued and tacked onto a wood molding. Felt piano parts are subject to attack by moths. As you can imagine, substantial damage can be done if moths are allowed to eat the felts. I will go further into moth protection in Chapter 6.

The string is wound around the *tuning pin* (8), which is driven into the *pinblock* (6). The pinblock is a laminated block of wood, attached underneath the plate (7). Laminated wood pinblocks have superior strength compared to the solid wood pinblocks used in old pianos. The laminations also help to keep the tuning pins tight. The importance of tight tuning pins is discussed further in chapter 3.

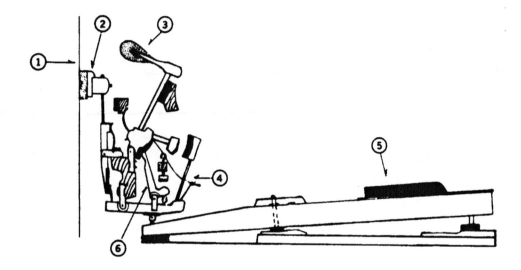

①STRING

②DAMPER

③HAMMER

④WIPPEN ASSEMBLY

⑤KEY

⑥JACK

#6 *Console Piano Action*

CONSOLE PIANO ACTION

The action of all vertical pianos function basically like that of the console piano. Console and upright pianos have the piano action sitting on top of the keys, with the hammers standing in an upright position. The action of the hammer striking the string is on the horizontal plane. On a grand piano, the hammers are lying down and strike the string on the vertical plane, allowing gravity to return the hammer to its original position. Grand actions repeat faster than verticals because of this design.

Although many of the basic parts in the console piano action differ from those of spinets and uprights, they generally serve the same purpose. The *key* (5) is depressed, contacting the *wippen assembly* (4). This forces the *jack* (6) to push up the *hammer butt*, and the *hammer* (3) strikes the *string* (1). When the key is released, the escapement parts (consisting of a *spring* and *bridle strap*) aids the hammer's return to its original position.

The escapement action parts become worn rather quickly and need replacement sooner than the other action parts. If a part is worn or out of adjustment, the hammer may "bobble" against the string when played. Usually, replacement of the bridle straps and a few minor adjustments will correct the problem. It is a simple procedure but should be done by a qualified piano technician.

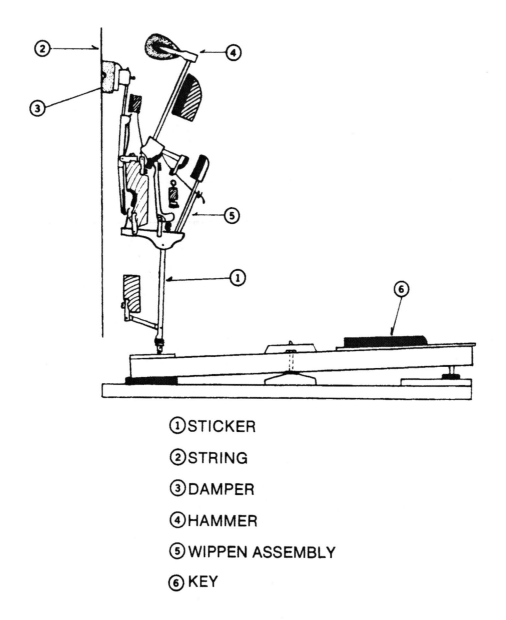

① STICKER

② STRING

③ DAMPER

④ HAMMER

⑤ WIPPEN ASSEMBLY

⑥ KEY

#7 Upright Piano Action

UPRIGHT PIANO ACTION

The upright piano action works the same way as the console piano action with one major difference, the *sticker* (1). The sticker sits on the key, and when the key is depressed, the force is transferred to the sticker, which is attached to the *wippen assembly* (5). The wippen then forces the *hammer* (4) to strike the *string* (2).

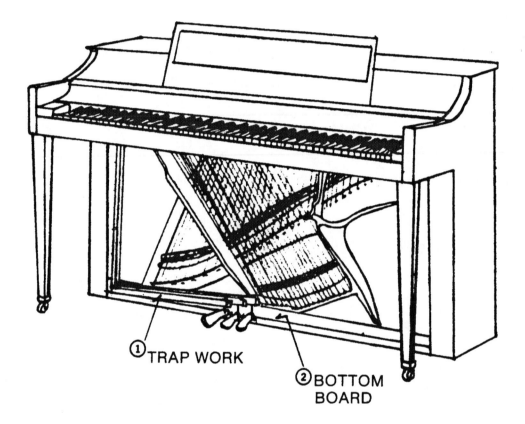

① TRAP WORK

② BOTTOM BOARD

#8 Vertical Piano with Lower Frame Removed

2

HOW TO PROPERLY
CLEAN A PIANO

WHY CLEAN A PIANO?

A general cleaning will enhance the appearance of your piano and prevent repair problems in the future. Sometimes a good cleaning is all that is needed to improve a piano's performance. Of course, you can pay a piano technician to clean your piano, but you can also clean it yourself. If you own a grand piano, see the sections on cleaning the strings and soundboard. If you own a vertical piano, first check the *bottom board* (2) of your piano by removing the *lower frame*, and examine the *trapwork* (1) area. The vertical piano's bottom board supports the pedals and the trapwork, which is located at the bottom of the piano.

If this is the first time that you have cleaned your piano, you may have to vacuum the trapwork area and wipe it down with damp cloth. After this initial cleaning, a light vacuuming should be all that is necessary to keep this area clear. If you live in the country or near wildlife, the trapwork is an essential area to clean and check regularly, or you could be in for a surprise.

Some of the older homes in New England contain the most beautiful and ornately carved upright pianos in the world today. The types of wood used and the craftsmanship that created these pianos place them in a class by themselves. Longstanding testimonials to an age past, these magnificent old pianos have been, more often than not, neglected for years. I received a call about "squeaking" in such a piano. Assuming the problem to be the pedals, I made sure to pack my oil, paraffin, and powdered graphite, the lubricants most commonly used to remedy this condition.

Armed with my cures, I arrived at a lovely

New England home. The owner, an elderly lady, directed me to the piano. Her granddaughter had an interest in learning piano and had started lessons a few weeks before. The woman explained that the squeaking occurred when her granddaughter practiced and that this was distracting to the little girl.

When I checked the tuning of the piano, it was obvious that it hadn't been touched for generations. The piano needed a pitch raising and remedial work to get it reasonably playable. It never ceases to amaze me that people can play pianos so out of tune without feeling discomfort. Before discussing tuning and repairs with the owner, however, I wanted to discover the cause of the squeaking. I checked each pedal numerous times without playing the piano. Squeaks can usually be identified by just working the pedals in this manner. Yet, there were no squeaks. This often happens. I receive a call or complaint about a malfunction in a piano, but when I arrive and check the instrument, everything seems to work fine. As soon as I leave, the problem suddenly returns. I haven't quite figured out whether this is my good fortune or the owner's bad luck. Consequently, I've learned to check problems thoroughly.

After telling the owner that the piano seemed to work fine and shrugging my shoulders, I removed the lower frame. To my surprise, there on the bottom board, to the right of the pedals, I discovered a little nest! Three little gray squirrels were curled up asleep, but the mother was nowhere to be seen. When the owner of the piano saw the squirrel's nest, she screamed so loudly that she nearly shook the house and I almost dropped the lower frame on my foot.

When things calmed down, I carefully removed the nest. The little animals squealed when they were awakened. Hence, we discovered the squeaking noises. I found a home for the squirrels outside, repaired the neglected piano, gave it a pitch raising, and a good cleaning.

The owner's granddaughter has long since moved away, yet the owner has learned to clean her piano frequently. As you can see, the bottom board and trapwork area are essential spots for you to check and clean regularly. Little squirrels, mice, and the like enjoy building their nests here. So keep it clean!

CLEANING SOLUTIONS

The question most frequently asked by piano owners is, "What do I use to clean my piano?"

There are several options available. The easiest, also the least effective, is a cloth slightly dampened with water. This can be used to dust the piano case, plate, and other areas where dust accumulates. Remember that piano strings are made of steel. Do not use a damp cloth on any steel parts, or they will rust. A damp cloth is adequate for daily or weekly dustings. However, to clean a piano thoroughly, which I discuss in detail further on, more effective cleaning solutions are recommended.

A cleaning solution popular with many piano technicians is two tablespoons of vinegar mixed well with one gallon of warm water. A mild solution of Ivory soap or any liquid ammonia detergent diluted with water can also be used. Spray cleaners are acceptable to use, but should be applied with a damp cloth rather than sprayed directly on to the piano. This method is the least complicated way of getting tough cleaning jobs done, but, here again, avoid getting any liquid or dampness on the strings.

CLEANING—KEYS

Since the wildlife conservation act was passed to protect the elephant population, it is illegal to manufacture pianos with ivory keys in the United States. Therefore, piano manufacturers have switched to plastic key tops. Some plastic key tops even have grains in them to simulate the look and feel of ivory keys.

Many older pianos still in active use today do, however, have the original ivory key tops. I remember a spinet with ivory key tops that I once tuned. The owner said she had cleaned the keys just before I arrived. She was a conscientious lady who was obviously proud of her piano. I was pleased to meet a person so concerned about maintaining her instrument, which appeared to be in excellent condition. I started to play the piano to check its tune and quickly jerked my hands away. I had experienced a queer sensation that made my flesh crawl. Then I noticed a sour smell and a dull, scummy film on the piano keys. The woman observed my reaction with surprise. When I asked what she had so painstakingly cleaned her keys with, she explained that she always cleaned them with milk!

If you own a piano that has genuine ivory keys, please do not clean them with milk.

The misconception that ivory piano keys must be cleaned this way has circulated long enough! It is my hope that this old rumor will be stopped here, once and for all. The only thing that milk does to ivory keys is make them stink and coat them with a sticky scum most unpleasant to the touch.

The best way to clean piano keys, both white and black, ivory and plastic, is with any of the cleaning solutions mentioned in the previous section. You must be careful not to use too much cleanser or water. Excess moisture can be harmful to the wood and felt bushings that the keys are mounted upon. Just a light touch of your cleaning solution applied to a damp cloth will clean the keys adequately. Be sure to dry the keys thoroughly after cleaning to avoid moisture damage and to give them that well polished look. And keep in mind that cleaning jobs will be simpler if you wash your hands before playing the piano.

CLEANING—CASE

A piano case (the exterior body of the piano) should be cleaned in the same way you would clean any fine piece of furniture, with a few exceptions. I recommend that you never use any type of aerosol furniture polish or, for that matter, any polish containing alcohol on your piano, as these will damage the finish. It is best to clean the case with a damp cloth or the water-vinegar solution mentioned earlier. After cleaning the case, the next step is to wax and polish it. Furniture paste wax is the best wax to use on a piano case. A good polishing will result in a glossy finish and will properly condition the wood. It will also help ensure your piano's long life and preserve its value.

For the piano pedals and brass hinges, any good quality brass cleaner does the job. Remember to follow the directions when using a brass cleaner. This will produce the optimum results and make the brass sparkle like new.

CLEANING—STRINGS

Piano strings are made of steel and are sometimes referred to as piano wire or music wire. Strings vary greatly in diameter (thickness) and length. The strings on a vertical piano are more protected from the environment than the strings on a grand piano. Vertical piano strings, therefore, require less cleaning. To look at the strings on a vertical piano, you lift the lid and remove the music shelf (see illustration #1 for the location of the parts). This gives you a good view of the tuning pins and the top part of the strings. By removing the lower frame, you will be able to see the bottom part of the strings and decide whether they need cleaning. If they do, it is best to let a piano technician do the work, as it involves removing the action from the piano. For a grand piano, however, you can clean the strings yourself.

The condition of the piano strings will affect its tone. If you see that your piano's strings are rusty, or dirty, it is time to clean them. The best procedure, especially on a grand piano, is to clean both the strings and the soundboard at the same time because the dirt and shavings from cleaning the strings will fall on the soundboard.

Do not use any cleanser when cleaning piano strings. Never use any oil on the strings or anywhere inside the piano. Oil will destroy a piano's tone and severely inhibit the piano's ability to stay in tune. I will explain later in the chapter on Protecting Your Investment how to prevent the formation of rust on the strings.

The best and easiest method of cleaning piano strings is rubbing them lightly with a fine grade of steel wool. Rub the strings back and forth, working out the rust until they shine. Use this method on bass strings, also. For cleaning the bass section, a heavier (coarser) grade of steel wool is recommended. Bass strings have a steel core with copper wound around it. The thick copper windings will rapidly disintegrate a fine grade of steel wool. As the note becomes lower, the copper windings become thicker, and the string increases in length for proper tone. Cleaning bass strings is a bit like polishing a copper penny. The more you rub, the more brilliantly they shine. Rubbing the strings back and forth disintegrates the steel wool, and on grand pianos these shavings fall on the soundboard. You can remove the shavings by blowing compressed air into the area or by cleaning the soundboard.

Compressed air or "shop" air, as it is often

called, is available in professional workshops. It is high pressure air suitable for a variety of applications and is generally not accessible to the piano owner. The exhaust from a vacuum cleaner is not as powerful as shop air and will not clean the soundboard sufficiently. The piano owner, therefore, should clean the soundboard by following the instructions given in the next section to achieve the best results. By properly cleaning the soundboard and the strings, the piano will look and sound its best.

CLEANING—SOUNDBOARD

The soundboard is the large board that forms the back of a vertical piano or the bottom of a grand piano. It is located behind the strings in vertical pianos, or under the strings in grands, and is attached to the plate. A soundboard is made of wood, usually spruce, and is about three-eighths of an inch thick. When a note is played, the soundboard vibrates and gives a more musical tone to the piano's voice.

The soundboard has a crown or gradual curve throughout the length of the piano. The crown may not be noticeable to the eye, but, if a piano soundboard has lost its crown, the ear can usually hear the difference. Pianos with flat soundboards have a dead sound and lack vibrancy. Besides helping to produce a musical tone, the soundboard aids in resisting the tremendous downward pressure exerted by the piano strings. The vibration of the soundboard, coupled with the sound of the piano strings, then, creates the musical quality of tone that we hear when playing a note.

Soundboards on grand pianos collect dirt and dust through the years, especially if piano lids are left open. Grand pianos need cleaning far more often than vertical pianos because dust and dirt build up more easily on a horizontal surface than on a vertical surface. It is, therefore, prudent to keep the lid and fallboard on a grand piano closed when the piano is not in use. Vertical piano soundboards rarely need cleaning, but, as mentioned in the *Why Clean A Piano?* section, the bottom board should be checked regularly.

When cleaning a grand piano soundboard, technicians use a soundboard steel. This is a flat, flexible piece of steel with a hole in one end. This steel is generally about twenty four inches long and can be purchased inexpensively at a piano store or from your piano technician. You must have this tool or a similar piece of spring steel to clean the soundboard. A vacuum cleaner will not reach down in between the strings to clean sufficiently. Compressed air blown across the area will remove some dust and debris, but it will not remove stains or other types of ground-in dirt.

Dampen a cloth with any of the previously mentioned cleaning solutions. Pull a portion of the cloth through the hole in the soundboard steel. Securely tie a string about twelve inches long to the other end of the cloth. Start cleaning at the extreme right end of the piano (treble section) and clean to the lower left corner beyond the bass strings. Following this method will allow you to gather the accumulated dust and dirt at the unrestricted area of the sound-board, to the left of the bass section, and remove the debris easily.

Read the following instructions carefully and study the pictures to grasp the process.

Insert the moist cloth, string end first, under the treble strings.

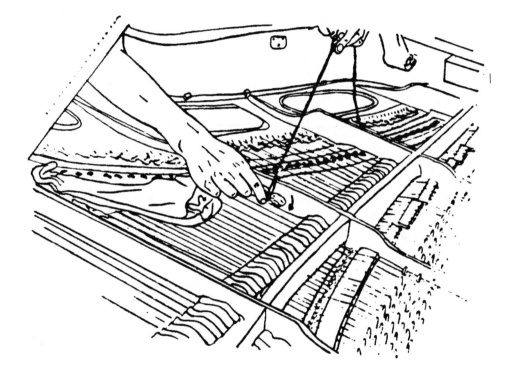

#9 Cleaning Grand Piano Soundboard—Step 1

Work the cloth under the treble strings with the soundboard steel. When the cloth is under the strings, grab the string you tied to the cloth and pull it up through the piano wire at the section break.

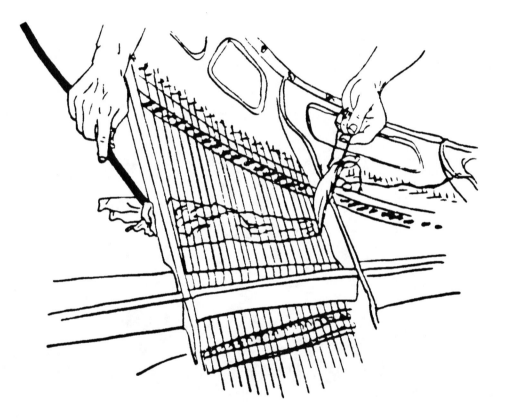

#10 *Cleaning Grand Piano Soundboard—Step 2*

Insert the other end of the cloth through the hole in the soundboard steel.

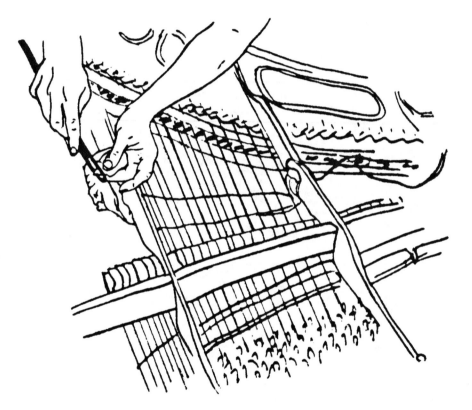

#11 *Cleaning Grand Piano Soundboard—Step 3*

Now you can push in one direction with the soundboard steel and pull in the other direction with the string. By working the cloth back and forth in this manner you will clean the soundboard. When you have reached the point that you can't clean any further with the present position of the soundboard steel, remove the cloth from the piano. Rinse the cloth in the cleaning solution. Squeeze out the dirt and rinse the cloth. Then, squeeze out the excess water and cleaning solution from the cloth and insert the whole arrangement as before. This time, start at the middle of the piano and proceed to the bass section.

You will be amazed how this cleaning will revitalize your piano. When you have finished, the soundboard will look like new, and the piano will sound more alive, too. The technique of working the cloth back and forth along the soundboard takes a little practice but can be quickly mastered.

A word of caution: always keep the cloth between the soundboard steel and the soundboard itself, to avoid unintentionally scratching the wood. Work all of the dirt and debris to the extreme bass side of the piano soundboard, beyond the last bass string, where it can easily be removed with a moist cloth. Piano technicians use this method and now you can use it. The result will be a clean soundboard that will enhance the beauty of your piano for years to come. The best part is, you can do it yourself and save money in the process.

HOW OFTEN SHOULD A PIANO
BE CLEANED?

A piano should be cleaned once every two to three years. This amounts to a lot of cleaning, but it has its rewards. The useful life of a properly maintained piano is fifty years under normal use before it needs a complete rebuilding. If a grand piano is neglected and not cleaned at all, dirt and debris will fall on the bass strings and settle on the soundboard, deadening tone. The dirt will also find its way into the action, causing friction between finely fitted parts, gumming up the motion. To avoid costly repair bills and, most important, to keep your piano working properly, clean it regularly. Regular and proper cleaning can make the difference between an increase and a decrease in your piano's value.

Most pianos, even small verticals, are rather large pieces of furniture and can collect a lot of dust and dirt. If not cleaned, a dirty piano can become an eyesore just like any other neglected piece of furniture. Most of my repairs begin with a complete cleaning of the instrument from top to bottom. Good piano technicians or mechanics will clean the item that they are working on before doing repairs.

The resale value of a piano (or anything, for that matter) can vary drastically between one that is maintained and one that is not. A clean piano looks cared for. People who are planning to sell a piano should clean it first to receive the best possible price for the instrument.

A customer asked me to appraise one of two pianos for sale. Both were grands that had belonged to a famous concert artist who had recently died. The pianos had served as practice instruments for the artist when she was at home. My client was interested in the larger of the two. From this information, it sounded like a simple appraisal. When I arrived, I thought that the home looked pretty small to have two grand pianos inside. I knocked on the door, and a nice, elderly lady answered and saw me in. The sun was out, and it took my eyes a few moments to adjust to the dark interior of the house. The curtains were drawn, and there wasn't much light. As my eyes adjusted to the light, I saw that the living room contained enough furniture, plants, and paraphernalia to fill a mansion, but, sure enough, hidden under all of this were two grand pianos. They were stuffed into the far corner of the room, side by side, and virtually buried under an assortment of items.

When I finally uncovered the piano that I was to appraise, I still needed more light to see the instrument clearly. After taking out my music lamp, turning it on, and setting it on the music shelf, I just about froze to the spot. There was a beautiful rosewood grand. It was completely covered with dust and dirt, but I could tell that the wood was rich rosewood. The tone of the piano was exceptional, and the action was signed by the man who built it. That piano, made in nineteen hundred, was a rare gem dulled by the darkness of neglect. I was dumbfounded by its beauty.

My job was only to appraise the instrument for my client, and it was none of my business how much was being asked for it, but I couldn't resist inquiring about the price. The lady was selling that incredible rosewood piano for a small fraction of its original value. I told her, if my client didn't buy the piano I would!

Of course, my client did buy the fine instrument. Happily, she contracted me to rebuild it. I refinished the rosewood case, repaired and regulated the action, and re-pinned and re-strung the harp. My client now has a wonderful instrument. The piano is worth at least ten times what she paid for it.

When preparing to sell your piano, don't hide it in a corner or bury it under needless junk. A piano should be a display item, placed in an open area and appreciated for its beauty as well as its tone. The rosewood grand now stands in the center its new owner's living room, which has a large picture window facing the street. All who pass by marvel at the beauty of this instrument. I suppose that this is justice done to a special piano that had been neglected for many years. Your piano can have a similar effect on visitors. If you keep it clean and shiny, people will notice even the most humble instrument. Part of the joy of piano ownership is just looking at it in the home.

3

WHY DOES A PIANO NEED TO BE TUNED?

STRINGS—DEFINED

A piano is a string instrument. The strings are made of steel and are under considerable tension. Most pianos have about two hundred to two hundred thirty-five strings, and each string exerts a tension of about one hundred sixty-five pounds. This translates to around eighteen tons of string tension on an mid-size piano. A nine foot concert grand piano supports about thirty tons of string tension.

The lowest eight strings of the bass section in a modern concert grand are single. This means that there is only one string for each note (key). The next twelve notes have pairs of strings, two strings for each key. All the rest of the notes have three strings each. When a key is played in the middle and treble sections, the hammer hits three strings simultaneously. Piano dampers prevent the note from ringing after release of the key. However, the top

twenty-one keys have no dampers because their vibrations are so small that it is not necessary to stop them.

String diameters differ in a piano. The deepest bass copper-wound string is approximately one-third of an inch in diameter (including the copper winding). Conversely, the highest steel strings of a piano are about one-thirtieth of an inch in diameter. Until the strings lose their elasticity, they try to pull back to their original relaxed state. A piano takes anywhere from two to five years of constant string tension at concert pitch to lose their elasticity and "settle." Then, they will be able to hold a tune for some time.

The illustration of a *Concert Grand* shows the positions of the basic piano parts. A concert grand piano is just under nine feet long (some concert grands are even longer). The piano *case*, or frame, (1) encloses the *plate* (2), *soundboard* (3), *pinblock, bridges* (4), and *tuning pins* (5). These basic parts serve to support the *strings* (6). If any of these basic parts change position, the tension of the strings changes, and the piano goes out of tune.

A piano's plate is made of cast iron and is usually painted a brass color. The plate supports much of the string tension and it exerts a force that helps preserve the *crown*, or curvature, of the soundboard. The pinblock is located under the plate and has the tuning pins driven into it. As mentioned, the pinblock is made of laminated wood for superior strength. Piano strings are coiled around tuning pins. When a tuner tunes a piano, he increases the tension on the strings by turning the threaded tuning pins tighter in the pinblock. Ideally, pianos should be tuned to concert pitch, commonly accepted as A440; meaning that A above middle C on the keyboard vibrates at 440 cycles per second.

If you don't have your piano tuned regularly, you are neglecting an extremely sensitive, not to mention expensive, instrument. The value of your piano decreases accordingly. If you decide to have your piano tuned after many years, a knowledgeable tuner and much care is required. Damage can be done to a piano that hasn't been tuned regularly. If a tuner tries to pull it up to pitch they can break many strings and even crack a plate. Consequently, a qualified tuner approaches a neglected piano with caution. It must be brought up to concert pitch gradually, which could mean a pitch raising and two more tunings in the next few weeks. Then the piano must be repeatedly tuned to stabilize the string tension. Four or more tunings may be necessary to stabilize a neglected piano or a new piano. A piano should be stabilized within a four week period so that it will hold its tune for a few months. In other words, a piano may require as much as a tuning per week to stabilize it at concert pitch if it is new or has been neglected. Since this can run into costly tuning bills, it pays to keep your piano in good tune throughout its useful life and avoid pitch raisings.

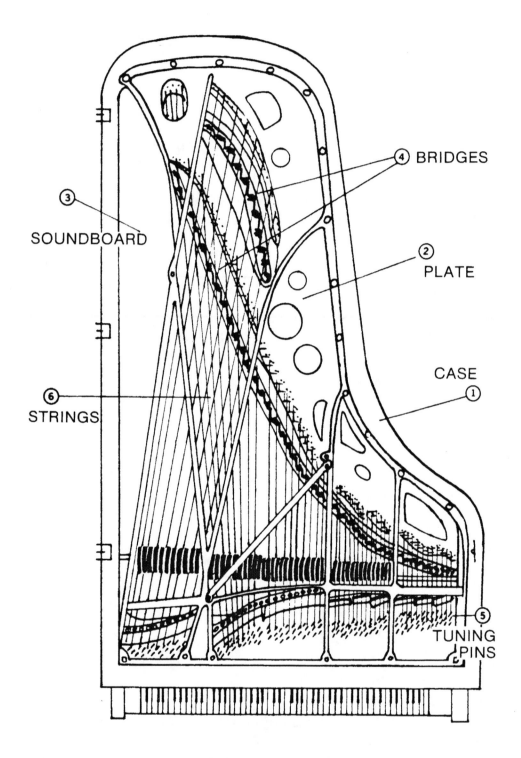

④ BRIDGES

③

SOUNDBOARD

② PLATE

CASE

⑥

STRINGS

①

⑤ TUNING PINS

#12 Concert Grand

STRINGS—STRETCH

Strings in new pianos rapidly stretch out of tune. They lose their tension and go flat owing to their elasticity. The problem is similar in older pianos needing a pitch raise of one-quarter to one-half tone to bring them to concert pitch. As soon as they are tuned, they immediately begin stretching flat. The tuner then must re-tune the piano soon to stress the strings properly and keep it at proper pitch.

After the first three years of a piano's life, its steel strings begin to "settle" and lose their elasticity. As we have seen, if it has been tuned regularly the strings will settle close to concert pitch. Then a six month or yearly tuning schedule will suffice for most pianos. If the piano has been neglected for the first years of its existence and has only been tuned once or so, it can settle as much as a half tone low. This means that when the note C is played, the note below it, in this instance the pitch for the note B, sounds. Practicing on a piano in this condition is especially harmful to the ears of young people starting piano lessons. It is important to train the ear at an early age so that the beginner can develop a true perspective of "relative pitch." A properly trained ear serves as an intuitive building block for many professional musicians.

The piano is designed to be tuned at concert pitch; this is the pitch where the piano will sound best. Maximum life will result for the instrument if concert pitch is maintained. On new and old pianos the strings are always stretching flat and require regular adjustment. When properly maintained strings have lost their elasticity and settled, the amount of adjustment needed decreases. Piano technicians say that a piano must be in tune to give it a fine tuning. If the piano has been tuned regularly and is close to concert pitch, the tuning pins only have to be turned a small fraction to bring the piano up to pitch. Slightly turning the tuning pin is the ideal situation for piano tuning, because small pin movements allow for fine work.

PINBLOCK

The superior strength of a laminated pinblock derives from its construction as well as its lamination. Slabs of wood are glued together with their grains running at different angles. A pinblock formed in this manner supports the tuning pins without cracking and creates the right amount of grip so that the tuning pins are tight but also loose enough to be turned smoothly when the piano is tuned.

The pinblock is fitted under the plate and attached with large screws. Ideally, the pinblock makes solid contact with the entire area of the plate. If part of it touches the plate and part does not, uneven string tension can result. A piano with uneven string tension will not hold a tune. The *Hardwood Pinblock* illustration shows the *string* (1) attached to the *tuning pin* (2), which is driven deep into the pinblock. The string's tension is absorbed by the tuning pin. As discussed, string tension in a piano is considerable. So a pin block is subjected to quite a bit of strain. The piano plate covers the entire pinblock but has been left out of illustration #13. Illustration #5—*Grand Piano Action*, shows how the pinblock is set in the piano with reference to the piano action and plate.

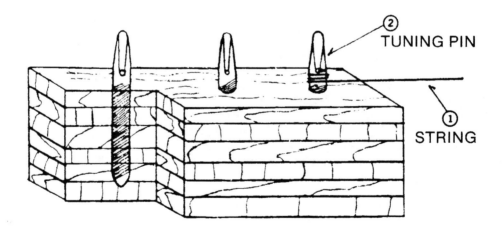

#13 *Hardwood Pinblock*

TUNING PINS

As illustration #13 shows, a tuning pin has a hole in its top portion and fine threads on its bottom portion. The piano string is inserted in the top hole and wound around the pin in a coil. The tuning pin's fine threads help it keep a tight grip when driven into the pinblock. First a hole is drilled through the plate and into the pinblock, and then the tuning pin is hammered into this hole. The threaded portion of the tuning pin creates added friction in the pinblock to aid in keeping the pin tight.

Most newer pianos have tight tuning pins. Often you can hear the pins "crack" in the pinblock as they are turned, in testimony to their tightness. As temperature, humidity, and time affect the pinblock, the pins gradually loosen. Constant string tension pulling on the pins contributes to their losing their grip in the block. When a tuner tells you that your piano has loose or slipping pins, he means that the tuning pins do not hold securely against the string tension. They either "skip" or turn rapidly. Loose pins are normal occurrences in many older pianos.

You can test your piano's tuning pin tightness by measuring the reverse torque of a pin. You install a special adaptor that fits over the tuning pin on an inch-pound torque wrench. Piano supply houses sell this adaptor. Then, you set the torque wrench at an ideal setting for the pin. Each manufacturer has different specifications for pin tightness, so check with your piano manufacturer for what the pin tightness should be. Age of the piano is a primary consideration when testing tuning pin torque. After you know the ideal setting, test the pin by turning counterclockwise, in the reverse direction to tightening the pin. If it holds, adjust your torque wrench to a lower setting. Keep testing and setting the wrench on lower and lower torque settings until you can smoothly turn the pin in a counterclockwise direction. This is the torque value for that pin. Test many pins throughout the piano to gain an average value.

For instance, in a Steinway concert grand, the pin torque values for a new piano should be around sixty inch-pounds. If you find that the average torque value is around forty inch-pounds, you can tap the pins in for more bite and the tuning should be stable. If you find that the average torque values are below twenty-five inch-pounds, then you must re-pin the piano, because it will not hold a tune.

The best cure for loose pins is replacement

with new pins one size larger. This means re-stringing and re-pinning a piano, a costly major repair. If the piano is not worth the investment to re-pin, you do have a few options. The technician can try to drive the tuning pins further into the pinblock by hammering them down with a tuning pin *setter*. If this does not tighten them enough to hold a tune, he can treat the pinblock directly with a chemical solution. The technician uses an eyedropper to drip the solution into the space around a tuning pin's base in the pinblock. The solution causes the wood to swell around the pin, forming a tighter fit between pin and pinblock. The solution should be applied at least three times and allowed to dry completely (which takes a day or so) between applications. If you have only a few loose pins, the technician can install copper sleeves into the pinblock and install a larger size pin. This often works, yet it irreversibly damages the pinblock.

Before installing a copper sleeve, I usually try superglue. This treatment is less abusive to the pinblock and has worked amazingly well. *CV Glue*, commonly called superglue, is available in three grades: thick, medium, and thin. I always use rubber gloves and have some CV solvent on hand if some accidentally sticks to my fingers. Acetone can be used as a solvent if no CV solvent is available. I try to store CV glue a cool dry place, because humidity will cause the glue to harden. I use the <u>thick</u> CV glue with <u>no</u> accelerator for loose tuning pins. If working on a grand piano, I remove the piano action and protect the keybed with a drop cloth. I gradually soak the pin bushing with the CV glue until the bushing has soaked up the glue to the tuning pin. Then I stop the glue application. Let it dry for 20 minutes. Afterwards, it should be ready to tune.

If these simple remedies are ineffective, then complete re-stringing and re-pinning may be your only option. Many tuners will not try the alternatives and will immediately urge a major repair. However, these simple remedies often work. In my experience, they work most of the time and can last for years. As a piano owner, you should be aware of them. Discuss the pros and cons of these remedies with your piano technician before agreeing to a costly repair job.

HUMIDITY AND TEMPERATURE

As mentioned, humidity and temperature effect all of the piano's parts. Extreme dampness and excessive heat are a piano's greatest enemies. In terms of a piano's tune, the part most effected by humidity and temperature is the soundboard. Although heavily coated with a protective varnish, the soundboard is still vulnerable to seasonal changes.

In spring the additional humidity in the air is absorbed by the wood in the piano. As moisture settles into the soundboard, its crown increases, creating more tension on the plate and strings, and the piano goes sharp in pitch. Conversely, in winter, with the drying heat of warmed rooms, the crown gradually decreases, and the piano goes flat in pitch. This increase in spring and decrease in winter is known as *seasonal pitch change*.

Humidity is much more significant for a piano's tune than temperature. Nevertheless, both change seasonally, and both affect pitch. Hence, piano technicians recommend tuning your piano at least twice a year, in the spring and fall.

HOW OFTEN SHOULD A PIANO BE TUNED?

A piano should be tuned as often as necessary. This depends entirely on the individual situation. If a piano is used as a piece of furniture and is rarely played, it should be tuned only once a year. If it is in a recording studio and is played every day, it should be tuned daily.

When a key is struck, the hammer pounds on the strings and quickly releases to the "checked," or rest, position. The more force exerted on a piano when it is played, the faster the loss of tune. Pounding will knock the strings out of tune on old and new pianos alike. However, if the piano has been maintained properly and if its strings have settled, it will withstand forceful playing and stay in tune relatively well.

During many concerts, a piano tuner waits in the wings (offstage). At intermission, the tuner re-tunes the piano and prepares it for the next part of the performance. Concert artists use such force when playing that few pianos will hold a tune satisfactorily. This should give you an idea of how quickly forceful playing can make a piano lose its tune and also of why concert artists' pianos need tuning more often than others.

Pianos in homes have less stringent requirements than pianos used professionally. The most extreme case for in-home tuning is a new piano, or one that has recently been pulled up one-quarter tone or more. Such an instrument needs tuning at least four times within the first twelve months to ensure that it remains at concert pitch and to give the strings a chance to settle correctly. After a new piano's first year, and for the next few years, it should be tuned every four to six months. Then it should be tuned according to its use. Generally, if a piano is used daily and is in good condition, tuning every four to six months should keep it in top form and in concert pitch.

During the summer months in the United States, there are many fine music camps for outstanding students who want to sharpen their musical skills. These camps provide instruction in all musical instruments as well as in band and orchestra. It is difficult for the camps to furnish enough pianos for two main reasons. First is the initial cost. Second is that camp buildings are generally constructed for summer use, three months at most, and not insulated as well as buildings intended for year-round use. It is not wise to leave pianos in such surroundings, but pianos are difficult to move. Most summer camps, therefore, do not invest in many pianos for their students. At best, they have only a few pianos, which can mean that students are severely curtailed in practice time.

One of the finest music camps in the country made a commitment to its piano students to provide enough pianos for practice. The camp started out as simply a teacher with a few piano students. Because it offered an adequate number of pianos both for practice and for concerts, it grew to be a respected music camp visited by outstanding musicians. There were gifted piano students from high school, colleges, and post-college levels. The piano teachers were carefully selected, and an attempt was made to match students and teachers in a manner calculated to bring out the students' best efforts. The music camp was located close enough to Tanglewood, Massachusetts, the summer home of the Boston Symphony Orchestra, to permit some of the professional artists who performed at Tanglewood to drop in. The artists would counsel students and give performances for the many music lovers who attended the camp's weekly concerts.

My father, the tuner-technician for the camp, followed a program to tune and repair each piano at the beginning of the season. The concert grand used in the weekly performances was tuned and maintained every week. It was a fine old grand that had been rebuilt several years before, and great care was given to its protection. It was kept locked except for practice and during concerts. When not in use, it was covered with heavy pads to protect it as much as possible from summer temperatures and humidity. However, age and the New England winters took their toll on the piano, and its tuning pins were no longer as tight and secure as they should have been. The instrument needed constant servicing to keep its tune for performances. Even then, it was touch and go.

A great American pianist was scheduled to appear at the camp one particular summer. He chose a Beethoven piece written expressly to demonstrate the capabilities of a piano's eighty-eight keys. The camp's old grand was tuned the day of the performance. Surprisingly, it held its tune quite well except for one note near the top of the treble section. As mentioned, each note in the treble section has three strings, and each string must be tuned exactly the same as the other two to produce a clear sound. Unfortunately, the note that didn't hold its tune was one that Beethoven liked and used constantly as the accentuating high note throughout the piece. Every time the artist hit the note, a resounding discord rang out. The highly trained musical audience did get to know when to expect that discord, and laboriously prepared for it each time, while my father cringed. My father, being the camp's tuner, felt terrible and to this day shudders when we laugh about the incident. Nonetheless, the artist was philosophical about it. Perhaps one of the marks of great pianists is that they understand the precarious art of piano tuning better than most.

THE DIFFERENCE BETWEEN A PITCH RAISING AND A NORMAL TUNING

Many people are confused about the difference between normal piano tuning and pitch raising. A normal piano tuning evens out a piano that is close to pitch. The strings are slightly stretched and the tuning pins "set." Normal piano tuning, under average conditions, should last four to six months. A pitch raising, on the other hand, is a wholesale jump in the piano's pitch and does not last long. Multiple normal tunings are required after a pitch raising to stabilize the piano.

New piano strings are highly elastic. A new piano should be tuned at least four times a year for the first *two* years to set the memory of the strings to proper pitch, thus stabilizing the piano. Pianos that are not tuned for a long time, or new pianos that have only been tuned once or twice in the first few years can go a quarter step, a half step, or even more flat. Some tuners leave such pianos at whatever pitch they find them and give the piano a normal tune. This leaves the piano dull, lifeless, and lacking brilliance. Since the piano is not up to pitch, it cannot be played along with other instruments. Pianists who practice on out of pitch pianos train their ears incorrectly, and get a false sense of tonal relationships. To tune a piano below concert pitch is irresponsible and little better than not tuning the piano at all!

The conscientious tuner, when confronted with a piano whose pitch is well below normal, will raise the piano to A-440 concert pitch. This is called a "pitch raising." Pitch raising usually requires a *double tuning* for the piano to hold pitch. The first pass, called a *rough* tuning, pulls the piano up to pitch. The second pass, called a *fine* tuning, stabilizes the piano strings.

Piano strings require a lot of stretching for pitch raising. The more the strings are stretched, the faster they will have a tendency to go out of tune. Newton's law of motion states, "For every action, there is an equal and opposite reaction." Strings pulled up to pitch will want to stretch out of tune very fast. So additional tunings within a few weeks following a pitch raising may be required. In addition, the piano owner should be prepared for one or more tunings within the next few months to completely stabilize the neglected instrument. Then, it should be tuned every four to six months with seasonal atmospheric changes to maintain the piano's pitch integrity.

The piano owner should seek out an honest and competent piano tuner who will tell them the truth about the condition of their piano. It costs more initially to bring the piano up to concert pitch, so many piano tuners do not mention it. Nonetheless, the rewards far outweigh the cost. It is most cost effective to properly maintain your piano when it is new, because it will eventually settle at concert pitch and change little with the seasons. Thus your piano will need less tunings over the long-term. This will save you money and maintain the value of your piano throughout its useful life.

WHY DO PIANOS GO OUT OF TUNE FASTER THAN WE EXPECT?

In the 18th century, when the piano was simple and less complicated, pianists could service their own instruments. They tuned their piano when needed, usually before every concert or practice session, just like a violinist. Yet, as piano action and design became more sophisticated, tuning and maintenance of the piano by the pianist became impractical. Today, the average piano owner is no longer able to tune their piano. They need a specialist. Considering the cost and availability of a trained piano technician, it became "practical" to tune and service pianos one to four times a year. Unfortunately, this new arrangement fostered unfounded myths, expectations, and misunderstandings.

As mentioned, the piano's many strings exert about two hundred thirty-five pounds of pressure on the plate and frame, translating to about eight tons overall. The plate, frame, bridges, pinblock, tuning pins, and soundboard support the strings and distribute the string's tensions throughout the piano. Anything that affects these parts will cause a change in string tension and make the piano go out of tune. Most piano technicians agree on three basic causes for piano tuning stability:

- loose tuning pins

- tensions not properly equalized during tuning

- climatic conditions

An experienced piano technician can easily detect loose tuning pins and suggest corrective measures. Also, a good piano tuner will "set" the tuning pins to properly equalize the piano's tensions during a tuning so that it will, hopefully, survive a performance. Yet, climate is beyond the piano technician's control. It only takes minutes of climate change to throw a piano out of tune. Hot stage lights often do it, as can slight humidity and temperature changes. Heating from the Sun, open doors and windows, cooling from air conditioners, house heating systems such as radiators, radiant floor heating, and baseboard systems, and many other external circumstances cause changes in temperature and humidity that "mysteriously" knock pianos out of tune. Most areas of the world have seasonal climate changes. Climate control systems such as Damper-Chaser systems can help. Yet, pianos still need a good tuning, be in good repair, and be in a relatively stable climate.

So, now that we know why a piano goes out of tune, how often do we tune it? How often depends on use and need. Pianos in concert halls are tuned before each concert and sometimes during intermission. Recording studios have their piano tuned before each session and have a piano tuner on duty during the recording session. Observing violinists, we see them tuning their four string instrument more than playing it. So, why do pianists consider it unusual that pianos, with more than two hundred strings, need frequent tunings? Ernie Juhn, RPT, in his article for the March 1989 *Piano Technicians Journal* answers this question. He writes, "Just as a car used as a taxi cab needs tires, brake lining, and lube jobs more often than do Sunday drivers, it is true that a piano used several hours a day needs a lot more frequent service than one used once a year to play *Jungle Bells*."

I usually recommend, as do most piano technicians, tuning a piano three to four times a year for *Jingle Bells* players. For teachers, musicians, and piano stores, every Monday and Friday. In the ten years that I worked for Stevie Wonder, I tuned the studio pianos for every recording session and every other day when he was not recording. For a piano teacher who uses the piano hours every day teaching twenty to thirty students a week, or a piano used by concert artists for twelve hours a day in a department store such as Nordstrom's, it is unreasonable to expect a tuning three or four times a year to be sufficient. It should be tuned as often as time and budget will allow.

EXPERT TUNING

A piano should be tuned by an expert. Many devices and many piano modifications have been designed to assist the piano owner in tuning his own instrument, but none have been successful. A novice has a hard time tuning a piano properly because tuning a piano is more about controlling the pin movements than hearing. Furthermore, a novice can damage a piano by overworking tuning pins.

In 1800 a piano builder named Hawkins developed mechanical wrest-pins that permitted tuning by varying pressure on piano pins. Other designers installed additional bridges in pianos to facilitate tuning. John Geib patented a buff stop to silence one string while another was being tuned. Streicher and Stein went one step further and modified the una corda pedal to mute selected strings so that other strings could be tuned. John J. Wise of Baltimore in 1833 invented a gadget that indicated the number of string vibrations on a dial. This idea eventually led to the tuning machines used by many piano tuners today. Despite these attempts to aid the amateur, the job of tuning a piano remained in the hands of professionals trained in the art. The secret to stable tunings lies not so much with the ears, but with the skill in manipulating the tuning pin. One of the greatest challenges in piano tuning is matching the strings that comprise a unison, or one note, exactly to each other. In an unstable tuning, one string will most likely go out of tune first, ruining the sound of the unison. Pleyel and Stanhope, prosperous conventional pianos manufacturers, designed a single string, or *unichord* piano, in an effort to allow the musician to tune their own instruments without having to match unisons. Yet after numerous prototypes, they abandoned their idea, because the hollow unichord piano sound was nowhere near as rich as a standard size piano with the correct amount of strings per note.

In the 19th and 20th centuries, piano manufacturers continued to develop an array of odd instruments that could be tuned by means of springs attached to metal tongues eliminating the need for special tools, adjustable metal rods used to produce the tones, and other revolutionary configurations. Some piano manufacturers tried to eliminate piano strings altogether. Yet when you remove the piano strings and produce sound electronically, you no longer have an acoustic piano. Experimental pianos such as the Rhodes electronic piano, manufactured in the 1970s, produced sound by neoprene-tipped hammers striking tuning forks. The sound was transferred to electronic pickup coils and heard through speakers. The Rhodes piano realized Pleyel and Stanhope's dream of a single string piano, yet these instruments still had to be tuned by technicians trained in electronic pianos. The owner could not do it themselves.

Today, the synthesized keyboard, a computer that requires no tuning, has replaced the electronic piano. Synthesizers are a whole new class of instrument. The *Korg SGproX*, for example, offers seven different scale types (temperaments) ranging from equal temperament, pure major, pure minor, Pythagorean, Workmeister, Kirnberger, and the traditional stretch temperament used on acoustic instruments. You can even blend them to create your own tuning!

Yet through it all, the acoustic piano design has stood the test of time and has remained relatively unchanged for over 100 years. It still requires tuning by an expert. A piano tuned by an expert will sound better and last longer than a piano tuned by a novice. The expert knows how to "set" a pin by pulling it slightly above the correct pitch and letting the string stretch back just the right amount, so that the note equalizes its tensions and "settles" at exactly correct pitch. A note played hard by a concert pianist stays in tune longer if it has been "set" and the string tensions stabilized. Many piano tuners are adept at this technique, which is just one of the differences between a good tuning and a mediocre tuning.

Quality tuning is an important factor in piano maintenance. All pianists, no matter what their level of accomplishment, enjoy the sound of a properly tuned piano. An old master tuner I studied under at Steinway & Sons Piano company in New York City told me, "A mediocre piano tuner can convince his customers to believe their pianos are in tune until those customers hear the sound of an expertly tuned piano. Then, that other tuner will lose a customer and you will gain one. Always strive to do your best." He encouraged me to reach for perfection with every piano I tuned, even though perfection is impossible. He said that striving for perfection would ensure that my tuning skill would continue to improve, and that, as a result, my clientele would grow through the years. I owe much to this great teacher's advice, and I try to follow it every day.

As a piano owner, use due diligence to find a piano tuner who is interested in giving you the most professional service available, and who cares about what he does. This is the tuner to contract for the job of maintaining your valuable piano.

4

VOICING AND REGULATION

PIANO PREPARATION

A piano manufacturer assembles and regulates pianos at the factory for delivery to the retail outlet. The factory does a pitch raising and roughs-in the regulation to make sure that everything works correctly. They bring their pianos up to a rudimentary condition for delivery to the store. Most manufacturers give a price discount to the dealers so they can pay a technician to prepare the piano for delivery to you, the customer. Before a piano is sold it needs to be regularly tuned to stabilize the strings and carefully regulated, a procedure known as piano *preparation.*

When shopping for a piano, it is important to ask if the instrument has been prepared or "prepped." Sadly, many dealers cut corners and sell pianos right out of the box from the factory. By selling the pianos in factory condition, the piano dealers pass on the cost of tuning and regulation to the customer. Many piano technicians are put in a difficult position as representatives of the store when they give a new customer their first tuning. They find the piano in poor regulation, needing a pitch raising and series of tunings in the first year. New piano owners often complain about the stiff touch and unresponsive action, thinking it is the fault of the piano and that it needs to be broken-in. In truth, it is a lack of piano preparation.

To avoid problems, the prudent piano buyer should have an independent, experienced piano technician examine any piano before they buy. Pianos are built to last generations. It is wise to have it checked by a piano technician before committing to a purchase. Then, if it needs work, you can negotiate a price discount to cover the labor *before* delivery.

WHAT IS GRAND PIANO ACTION REGULATION?

The grand piano action is that part of the piano that transfers the striking force from the key to the string. The action is the heart of every piano. Action regulation determines piano touch and tone.

An analogy can explain piano regulation. Let's say you buy a new car. Do you pay $20,000 for the parts of the car, or do you pay $20,000 for the timing to make the car run? What good is $20,000 worth of parts if the car doesn't run? Timing makes the car run. So it is with pianos. Regulation sets the timing of the piano so it will function at peak performance.

Grand piano regulation involves a series of complicated steps with many adjustments in each step. The more precise the regulation adjustments, the better the results. The piano technician cannot simply follow a checklist, go step by step, and arrive at the best settings for a particular piano, because each piano presents unique challenges and different solutions.

The master class for piano technicians taught by Yamaha called *Grand Action Regulation in 37 Steps* speaks to the next important point. It states:

"Where do we do the work? In the home or at a shop? There is no argument against a shop in the life of every piano technician. It is true that the shop is essential for major repairs, for rebuilding, and for any preliminary work needed to be done on the regulation job. However, it is just as true that it is possible to do more accurate regulation at the piano than at the bench. In the shop, it is impossible for a technician to duplicate the exact situation that exists in a piano. Even with the care and effort necessary to make a perfectly flat work bench for the shop, one finds that not all keybeds are flat. How do we set up to duplicate the string height of the piano back at the shop? Usually the target we use at the bench for the string height is a straight board, but the string line in each piano varies from a straight line. It depends on the shape of the cast iron plate which, in cooling, takes on a slightly different shape from one plate to the next. The only practical way to get the exact set of conditions existing in a particular piano is to go to that piano and work within the conditions found there. Regulation as we [at Yamaha] view it, should be thought of as customizing an action to perform best in a particular piano."

You, the customer, should be aware of this essential point when contracting a piano technician to regulate your grand piano. If the technician comes to pick up your piano action for regulation, takes it to his shop for a few weeks, and throws it back into the piano with few or no adjustments, you know the job is not finished.

What makes regulation so demanding is the circular nature of the work. To do the job right, every adjustment requires many small corrections to elements already set as other elements are brought into line. The piano technician goes round and round in a circular maze of precise regulation settings. Each painstaking pass brings him closer to solving the problem of how to achieve the best piano touch and tone. This repetitive process tests the piano technician's character. He must have tenaciousness tempered with patience to persist until the job is done. By any standards, piano regulation is challenging work.

VOICING

The tonal quality of a piano can be changed by properly shaping and conditioning the hammers. Technicians call this voicing. Piano hammers are made of felt, pressed and glued around a wood molding. The different layers of felt on a hammer can be identified by their different colors. After the felt layers are glued and tacked to the molding, the hammers are conditioned before they are installed in the piano. Domestic piano manufacturers use a lacquer mixture to harden and condition the felt. A word of caution is needed here. Lacquer can only be used on American hammers made with American felt. European hammers use European felt and do not condition their hammers with a lacquer mixture. In fact, you should never, under any circumstances, use lacquer on European hammers such as those manufactured by Renner. Lacquer will render these hammers worthless, because they will no longer be able to be voiced correctly.

New piano hammers are conditioned to what I call the downside of neutral. As a new piano is played the hammer felts compress, causing the piano's tone to become more brilliant. Exactly how much new hammers will compress cannot be anticipated because piano felt is unique. After the first few years of constant use the hammers settle and no longer compress. As the piano is played the hammers begin to retain the impression of the strings they strike. This is the time to have your piano voiced to your own particular needs.

Many contemporary artists prefer a brilliant tone while most classical artists enjoy a rich, mellow tonal quality. No matter what your musical tastes, voicing will make the piano's tone cleaner and more dynamic. If the hammers are not voiced, the strings will cut through the soft hammer felt and the hammers will deteriorate more rapidly than necessary.

Piano voicing has three basic steps. First, the hammers are filed and shaped with sandpaper. This creates properly curved surfaces to strike the strings when the piano is played. Correct hammer curvature helps to prevent string breakage. If the tone needs to be brought up, American hammers are hardened with a weak lacquer solution. Properly hardening them brightens the piano's tone and at the same time conditions, preserves, and protects the hammers from premature wear. European hammer felts are already hard, and after filing, you proceed to the last step. The hammers are repeatedly pierced or needled with a voicing tool to refine and even the piano's tone.

Most pianos should be voiced when the hammers show wear. Pianos used for performances, teaching, and in recording studios require voicing much more often than pianos in homes because they are played long and hard. A dull, lifeless tone is an indication that a piano needs to be voiced. Voicing will dramatically enhance a piano's tone and increase your enjoyment of its sound.

THE DIFFERENCE BETWEEN PIANO VOICING AND TONE REGULATION

When a piano functions its best, it produces optimal tone. To get a piano functioning its best, the piano action must be regulated before it is tuned and voiced. Voicing a piano without regulating it first is akin to putting the cart before the horse. It is a waste of time and money. Action regulation sets the timing of the piano so it will function at peak performance and produce its best tone. Without proper action regulation, the piano coughs, chokes, and stumbles like a car needing a tune-up.

As mentioned, piano action regulation involves a series of precise steps with many adjustments in each step. The better the technician performs the regulation adjustments, the smoother the piano plays and sounds. For this reason, many piano technicians call piano action regulation "tone regulation." One of the finest piano tone regulators I know said, "Tone regulation is to voicing as pitch raising is to tuning."

A piano needs a normal tuning when it is close to pitch. A normal tuning adjusts individual notes within a piano *already* up to pitch. If a piano is not tuned for a long time, it can slide very flat in pitch throughout.

These pianos need a pitch raising. Pitch raising is a wholesale jump in pitch for every note in the piano. Similarly, tone regulation is a wholesale jump in putting the action close to where it needs to function for best tone. Voicing, like tuning, adjusts the sound of individual notes in relation to those around it.

After the piano action and case are tone regulated, it can be finely tuned. When the pianist plays it, the piano's true sound quality will shine through. Now the piano can be safely voiced. One word of caution, a piano should not be voiced until the hammers and felts are broken-in, usually a minimum of one year for new pianos with average use.

When the time finally comes to voice the piano, the pianist meets with the technician to discuss it. A piano is voiced to only one person's taste. The pianist works with the technician, sometimes note by note, to perfect the voicing.

Piano technicians use various techniques to get the desired results. Often, the piano hammers need filing and reshaping for the desired tone. The technician may needle the hammers to arrive at the tonal quality desired by the pianist. The technician may use chemical treatments to brighten the tone on hammers manufactured in the United States. As we have seen, all hammer felt is created equal. Some hammers are manufactured in the United States and some in Europe. Remember, chemical treatments should never be used on European hammer felt or you run the risk of ruining the hammers. Obviously, the technician must be experienced in the subtleties of voicing procedures and tone regulation, or he runs the risk of undoing the action regulation work he labored so long to accomplish.

Whether you have a grand piano or a vertical piano, its tone can be dramatically improved by tuning, voicing, and tone regulation.

5

MINOR REPAIRS YOU CAN DO YOURSELF

ADVISORY

The repairs covered in this section pertain mainly to vertical pianos and can be accomplished without removing the piano's action. A willingness to get the job done and a keen eye are the most important tools you'll need.

To repair a grand piano, one must first remove the action and this can be tricky. An inexperienced person is likely to depress some piano keys accidentally raising some piano hammers (especially the highest treble or lowest bass keys) while sliding the action out of the case. Hammers easily snap off the shanks when they hit the bottom of the pinblock. Hammer repairs require special tools. To avoid complications it is best to call a qualified piano technician for grand piano repairs.

STICKY KEYS—BASIC

There are five common causes for sticky keys.

1) a foreign object inside the piano

2) warped piano parts

3) key bushings too tight

4) one key interfering with the next

5) misalignment

Of course, many things can disrupt a piano key's proper operation. Yet based on my experience, the problem will usually turn out to be one of these five. You can remedy sticky keys if you approach it in a systematic way. Carefully check the key or keys that are not functioning properly. If a careful examination of the outside of the piano reveals nothing out of the ordinary, such as a foreign object lodged between the keys or the white keys sticking on the keyslip (see illustration #14), then a more critical look at the inside will be necessary. At this time, you can usually narrow the cause down to one of the five possibilities given above, which are discussed in detail in this section. However, even sticky keys can have exotic or bizarre causes.

I remember receiving a call from a man who made an appointment for a tuning and repair of his grand piano. He said that he had been having some problems with a few sticky keys. When I arrived at his piano, I tried to play it to check the tune. I quickly realized that there were more than just a few sticky keys. Some notes sounded, but the keys stayed down. Others played sluggishly, and many didn't play at all. It seemed to me that I was looking at a piano that had every symptom in the book, and a few more. I began to realize that my look at his piano could turn into a major rebuilding job, which might take months to complete.

I removed the fall strip and tried to dislodge the fallboard, the last part to remove before sliding the action out of the piano, but it would not budge. I checked the fallboard carefully and saw no reason why it shouldn't just come out, and so I forced it, risking parts

breakage. The fallboard sprang out with a vengeance, propelled by a virtual flood of assorted nutshells.

Once this outpouring had settled on my lap and the floor, I surveyed the situation inside the piano. The action was still buried under a mountain of shells shoved between the pinblock and top stack. Every available nook and cranny around the action had a shell, or shell fragment, stuffed into it. I was amazed any notes worked at all. The nutshells so restricted the action that some hammers couldn't even move to strike the strings. Most of the shells were empty, and many had been emptied through little holes in the side, leaving the shell intact. The inside of the piano was obviously used as a den by some varmint.

I showed the owner my discovery and asked him if he was in the habit of stashing nuts inside his piano. He was a little set back by my question. Nonetheless, we had a good laugh about it. He said that no one had been near the piano for quite some time. Except for the shells inside the instrument, there was no evidence of invaders outside the piano. We wondered where the little critters found such a bountiful supply of nuts. Yet we did not have to look far to locate the source. The coffee table next to the piano had a large crockery bowl full of nuts. The owner and his wife each thought the other was enjoying the nuts and regularly replenished the bowl. We surmised that mischievous chipmunks stole the nuts from the bowl, stashed them, and enjoyed nightly feasts inside the piano.

I removed the debris and cleaned the piano thoroughly. It took the better part of the day. When I was finished, we were both happy that this was the piano's only problem. The owner immediately removed the bowl of nuts from his music room.

Even though this is an exceptional sticky key problem, you may come across something that you can repair by yourself if you take the time to investigate. It is, at least, worth your while to try and identify the problem. A quick look may save you money. If, after a careful examination of the keys along the lines covered in the following pages, you can't find the cause of the malfunction, then it is time to call a piano technician.

STICKY KEYS—INSTRUCTIONS

Sticky keys are generally the most common complaint of pianists and piano owners. The first step in correcting the problem is to identify the cause. As you read these instructions, locate the parts in your piano as they are mentioned.

Closely examine the key that is sticking. If you find only white keys sticking and black keys working fine, the problem might be a warped *keyslip*. The keyslip is a strip of wood that runs the length of the *keybed* and protects the keys. Keyslips tend to warp, even on new pianos. When the key is depressed, the warped part of the keyslip catches the front of the white key and holds it down. This is a common problem, and it is approached similarly on both grand and vertical pianos.

Insert a *shim* such as a matchbook cover, business card, or any small piece of cardboard between the keyslip and *keyblock* at each end of the keyboard. Shims create more clearance between the keyslip and the key front and will often solve the problem. If you still have sticking white keys only, the keyslip must be removed, and shims placed all along the base of the keyslip. Make sure that the shims do not interfere with the movement of the key. Refer to illustration #14 for exact shim placement.

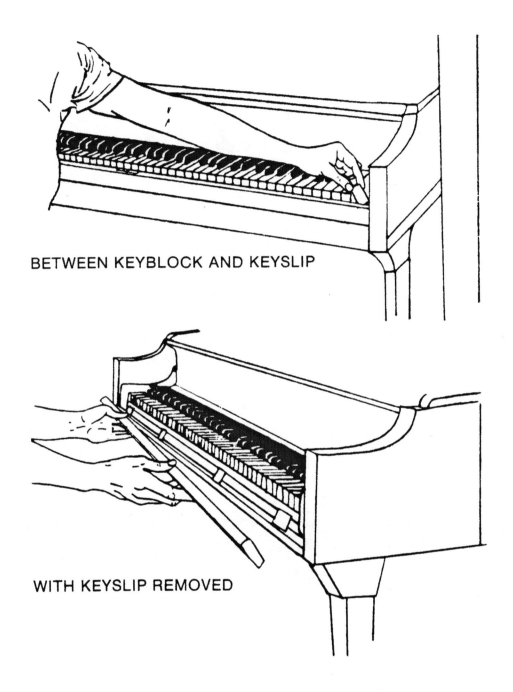

BETWEEN KEYBLOCK AND KEYSLIP

WITH KEYSLIP REMOVED

#14 *Shim Placement*

Some piano manufacturers have anticipated this common problem. Many new vertical and grand pianos have adjusting screws (1) mounted into the keybed (2) to make spacing easier. After you have removed the keyslip, check the keybed for screws of the type shown in illustration #15. If no screws are present, you can put in some small adjusting screws directly into the keybed at the friction points. Then, you can carefully unscrew them until the proper clearance between the keyslip and the keys is achieved. I recommend turning them about one-half turn and checking the key clearance. If there is not enough clearance with the keyslip attached, then remove the keyslip again, and turn them another one-half turn. Turning the screws out too much is not desirable, because it can make reinstallation of the keyslip difficult.

After making all the necessary adjustments, reattach the keyslip. There should be sufficient clearance for the white keys to function properly.

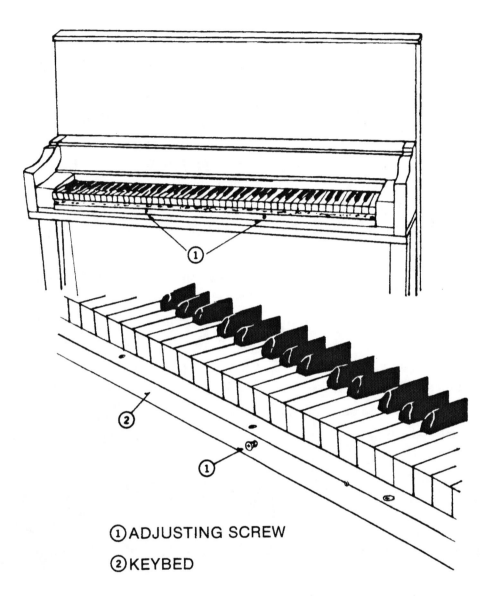

① ADJUSTING SCREW
② KEYBED

#15 Modern Vertical Piano with Keyslip Removed

If the problem is not a warped keyslip, then it is time to look further. Raise the lid, and fold it back. Prop it open with a lid support block or against the wall behind the piano. It is a good idea to have a cloth between the lid and the wall to prevent damage to the piano finish.

Next, remove the music shelf. Usually there are two screws (pins) that attach the music shelf to the sides of the piano. Once these are out, the music shelf should slide toward you on a wood track or brass guide pins. Slide it gently out of the piano and set it aside.

Then, remove the fallboard. Fallboards come in a variety of different styles. As a general rule, look to determine how the fallboard is attached to the frame, and remove the screws holding it in place. Be sure to remember where all the screws came from when you put them aside.

The last part to be removed for the vertical piano preliminary inspection is the fall strip. It is usually attached by one or more nuts in the center section of the keyboard, and by two screws, one on each end. Remove the screws and nuts, and store them safely aside with the other screws. Now lift the fall strip out of the piano.

When you have removed the music shelf, fallboard, and fall strip, you have completed the most difficult part of correcting most sticky key problems. Look for the obvious. First, try to see how the piano key works. Press it down, and watch how the note plays. Notice how the key rocks on its *balance pin* (see illustration #16), and how close one key is to the next. By observing the movement of the piano key, you will usually be able to see whether anything like a penny or other small object has become lodged between the keys, causing sluggish response when played. Maybe a pencil has fallen into the action and is interfering with the key's ability to strike the string. These obvious foreign object problems occur regularly and can render a key useless. If this is the case, carefully remove the object, and your problem is solved. Many piano technicians have done "brilliant" repair jobs by removing a pencil or a lodged penny stuck between two keys.

Piano keys are made of soft wood, usually sugar pine, which absorbs moisture easily when a piano is subjected to high humidity. This causes swelling of the wood and the *felt bushings* that surround the balance and *front rail pins*, which hold the key in place. When a key's bushings are too tight, it is slow to repeat, and is referred to as a sluggish key. To correct this problem, you must increase the clearance between the pin and the bushing itself. You do this by squeezing the felt bushing on the key. But first, you must remove the key from the piano.

To remove a key, lift up the end of the key closest to you and gently pull the back of the key out of the piano. Notice how the key rides on two pins, a balance pin (2) and a front rail pin (3). Each pin has two separate bushings on each side of it. One bushing is in the center of the key and surrounds the balance pin (see illustration #17), while the other is located under the area where you strike the key and surrounds the front rail pin (see illustration #16). If they are too tight, these bushings must be opened wider to give greater clearance for the pins. To open the bushing, gently squeeze it with *easing pliers*. If easing pliers are not available, small, smooth surfaced, flat-billed pliers available at most hardware stores will do the job. Be careful not to squeeze too much, as this would make the key too loose. Too much side play is not desirable and would make regulation uneven.

Reinsert the key in the same manner that it was removed, and check again for sluggishness. If the bushing is still too tight, repeat the process until the correct side play is achieved. The proper clearance between bushing and pin is one that allows for unrestricted motion with as little side play as possible. The measurement is taken by depressing the key completely and then moving it from side to side. The adjustment is correct when there is a small, but definite, movement. The actual measurement given by the factory is three tenths of a millimeter. This would be difficult to measure exactly, but can be felt as a slight free movement as the key is moved from side to side. (taken from: *Piano Technology the Yamaha Way—Grand regulation in 37 Steps, A Master Series*)

Sometimes the keys themselves become slightly warped, causing friction between two neighboring keys. To correct this problem, make sure that the warped key is centered as much as possible. Technicians bend the balance pin to align a key properly. Use a screwdriver with the palm of your hand to bend the pin (see illustration #17). If the key is centered, but still rubs against its neighbor, remove the key, and sandpaper the contacting surfaces. Replace the key, and again check for clearance.

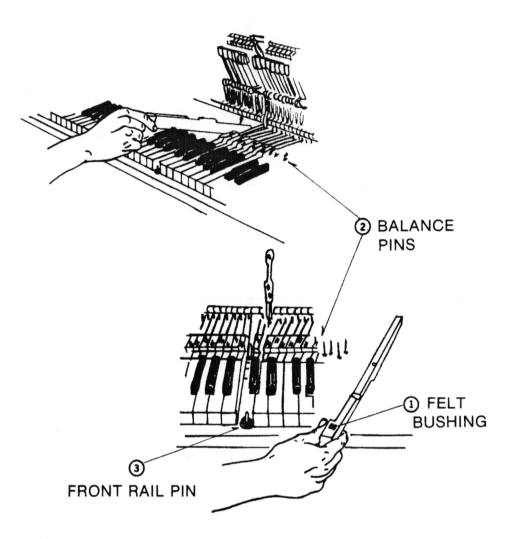

② BALANCE PINS

① FELT BUSHING

③ FRONT RAIL PIN

#16 *Piano Key—Removal and Bushings*

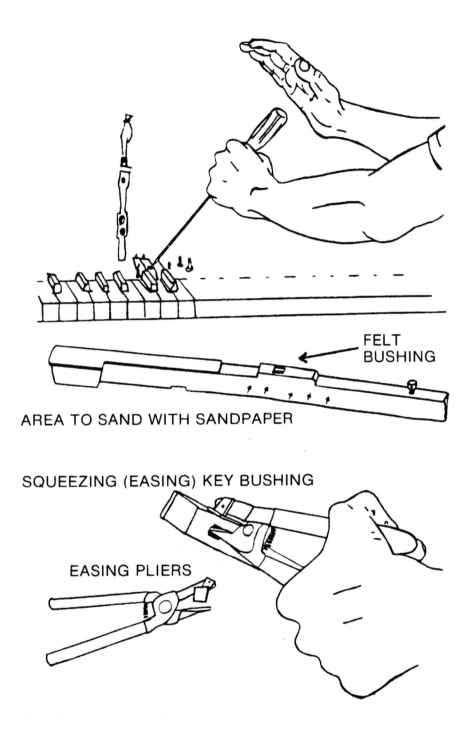

FELT
BUSHING

AREA TO SAND WITH SANDPAPER

SQUEEZING (EASING) KEY BUSHING

EASING PLIERS

#17 *Key Easing and Centering*

These are the most common solutions to the most common problem: sticky keys. If none of these suggestions works for sticky or sluggish keys, your problem may be of a more serious nature. This is the time to reassemble the piano and call an experienced piano technician. However, most sticky key complaints that I've handled turned out to have one of the simple causes.

When reassembling the piano, start with the fall strip, next the fallboard, the music shelf, and lastly, close the lid. Work in a careful and organized manner, and you won't have any difficulties.

STICKY KEYS—SPINET PIANO

As described in the *Piano Types* section, spinet pianos look like small console pianos but have one important difference, a drop action. The action doesn't sit on top of the keys; it rests below them. Examine the illustrations in the *Piano Types* section and in this section, and you will see how the action sits in the piano case.

Sticky keys on a spinet piano can originate from any one of the previously mentioned general sticky key problems, or from the particular spinet problem, the *lifter elbow* (7). Many spinet elbows were made of plastic during World War II when plastics were experimental. Unlike plastics made today, this type of plastic deteriorates, becomes brittle, and falls apart. Plastics today are much more advanced and will last longer than wood. Yet most spinet pianos were manufactured during the 1940s and 1950s. You can count on these pianos needing new elbows. The plastic becomes so brittle that you can crush it with your fingers. When a key on a spinet piano will not play and remains in the down position, 99 times out of 100 it has a broken elbow made from outdated material.

To determine if a broken elbow is the cause, you must remove the lower frame and look inside the piano action. In the *Spinet Piano*

Action illustration #18, there is an enlargement of a modern *spinet replacement elbow* (7) made from plastic. It can be inexpensively bought at a piano supply store or from your piano technician, and is easy to install.

Carefully remove the broken elbow by crushing it with pliers; usually it will break easily. (The plastic fragments can be cleaned up later.)

Screw the *lifter wire* (5) into the new elbow. Without removing the pin, snap on the replacement elbow, and insert the lifter wire carefully into the key. Adjust the wire to give some lost motion in the piano key so that the hammer shank can rest against the rest rail. With the key in this position, it will work correctly.

In the past, spinet pianos were popular as beginner pianos because of their low cost. If you study the drawing, you will notice that the action works similarly to that of most uprights. However, because the action is below the keyboard rather than above it, and because the lifter wires block access to the action, spinets are difficult and costly to repair. If any problem causes a key to malfunction other than broken lifter elbows, it is recommended that you call a piano technician for service.

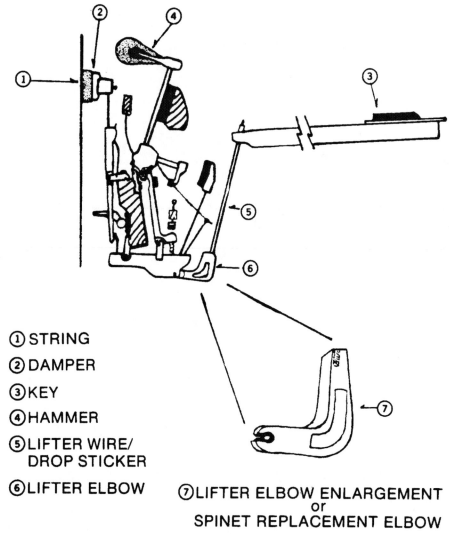

① STRING

② DAMPER

③ KEY

④ HAMMER

⑤ LIFTER WIRE/
   DROP STICKER

⑥ LIFTER ELBOW

⑦ LIFTER ELBOW ENLARGEMENT
   or
   SPINET REPLACEMENT ELBOW

#18 *Spinet Piano Action*

PEDALS—FUNCTION

The *trapwork* is the pedal assembly in vertical pianos. In grand pianos, the pedal *lyre* supports the pedal assembly. Older pianos have two pedals, but most have three. In vertical and grand pianos, the right pedal is the *sustaining* pedal, sometimes called the loud pedal. When it is depressed, all of the dampers lift at once. You can find the location of dampers in the piano action illustrations. The dampers mute the strings which prevents the strings from sounding until the note is struck. As the hammer is struck, the dampers lift off the string allowing it to ring until the note is released. When all of the dampers are lifted at once by pressing down on the sustaining pedal, all of the notes played will continue to ring until the pedal is released.

The left pedal is called the *soft* pedal. In vertical pianos this pedal moves all the hammers closer to the strings. This repositioning of the hammers reduces the distance they travel and reduces their force in striking the strings. The less the striking force, the softer the resulting note. In most grand pianos, the left pedal shifts the whole keyboard and action to the right, changing hammer alignment to the strings. Three strings comprise a treble, middle, and high octave note. As mentioned earlier, the strings for each individual note are called a *unison*. When the action is shifted by the left pedal, the hammer strikes only two strings in the unison, creating a softer tone. Because the hammer's position to the strings is changed, the proper term for the soft pedal is the *una corda* pedal.

Most modern pianos have a third pedal. The third pedal is between the loud and the soft pedals and is called the *sostenuto* pedal. When this pedal is depressed on grand pianos, the notes played just before activation of the pedal will sustain (continue to ring) after the keys are released. Any notes played after the pedal has been depressed will not sustain but will sound normally, or *staccato.* In many vertical pianos the middle pedal is used for sustaining only the bass notes. When it is depressed, all the dampers rise off the strings in the bass section. The pianist can strike a chord in the bass section and play with both hands in the treble without sustaining the sound of the treble notes. This phenomenon is sometimes referred to as the *third hand* effect.

In other vertical pianos, depressing the middle pedal positions a thick strip of felt between the hammers and the strings throughout the length of the piano. This felt strip, attached to a bar hung inside the cabinet, muffles the sound on every note of the piano. If you live in an apartment or practice in an area where your playing might disturb your neighbors, this is a good pedal function to have as it allows you to practice quietly without the piano's full voice. When the third pedal has this feature, it is called the *practice* pedal.

SQUEAKY PEDALS—GRAND PIANO

Most of the annoying squeaks in a piano come from the pedal assembly or the noise of a grand action shifting during the soft pedal's activation. Piano supply houses offer technicians a dizzying myriad of solutions for squeaky grand keybeds and pedals; fancy powders, high-tech sprays, wood soaking solutions, special graphite crayons. I have tried them all with little success. Far and away, the best and safest cure for squeaky keybeds is paraffin; petroleum based, unscented candle wax. Piano technicians used this before the development of all the fancy high-tech offerings, and it is still the best, safest, and longest lasting lubricant to silence a determined squeak between two wood surfaces.

Grand piano pedals go out of adjustment through normal use or when disassembled in moving a piano. The pedal lyre in grand pianos often creates squeaks when it works loose. Be sure to check the bolts and nuts that connect the lyre to the piano first. Simply tightening these nuts or bolts, as the case may be, will most often solve pedal squeaks. To adjust the pedals, all you have to do is look at the setup and turn the appropriate *adjusting nut* (3) to lengthen or shorten the *connecting rod* (5). You eliminate excess play (lost motion) in the pedal of a grand piano by turning the adjusting nut to lengthen the connecting rod. Sometimes the *leather pads* (4) create a squeak when the pedal is used. It is best to lubricate the leather surfaces with powdered graphite, ordinary pencil lead. Never use oil on pedal contact points with leather or cloth bushings.

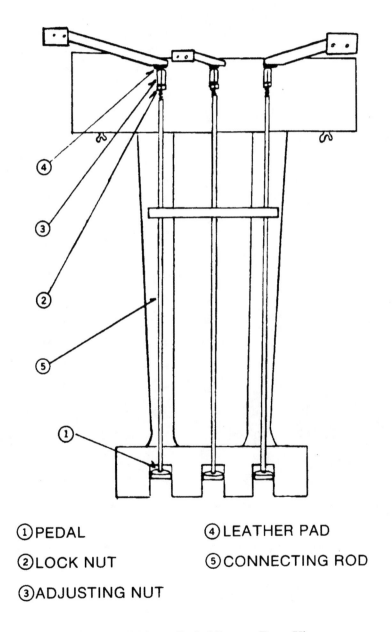

① PEDAL　　　　　④ LEATHER PAD

② LOCK NUT　　　⑤ CONNECTING ROD

③ ADJUSTING NUT

#19 Grand Piano Pedal Lyre—Rear View

SQUEAKY PEDALS—VERTICAL PIANO

It is always a good idea to clean the trapwork as discussed in the cleaning section of this manual before doing any adjustments. Pedals on vertical pianos are adjusted in a similar manner to grand pianos. The *adjusting nuts* (4), situated in the bottom of a vertical piano, are turned to adjust the *trap levers* (1). However, you must first remove the lower frame. It snaps off easily. Next, work the pedals to locate the squeak. If it is noticeable, apply a silicone based lubricant to the metal parts that interact.

Sometimes the pedal *dowels* (2), which connect the trapwork to the action, squeak. Pedal dowels are usually made of wood. Through the years the wood can warp. A warped dowel rubbing against the frame of the piano causes a squeak whenever the pedal is used. The best lubricant to use in this case is paraffin. Rub an unscented candle on the contacting wood surfaces and you will eliminate the squeak. If the warp in the pedal dowel is severe and prevents the pedal's proper function, the dowel should be replaced. Replacing a pedal dowel on a vertical piano requires finesse. If you have any doubts about your ability to ease the dowel back into position, ask for the assistance of an experienced piano technician.

STRANGE PIANO NOISES

When you play a piano, you expect to hear pleasant musical sounds. Yet sometimes you hear something far from musical such as zings, clicks, squeaks, groans, knocks, rattles, buzzes, whooshes, and scratches. Sometimes odd sounds seem to come from deep within the piano and sometimes these strange noises float at you as if from another dimension. Odd piano sounds are some of the most difficult things to diagnose and correct. Piano technicians usually run away from a piano with strange sounds as fast as possible and pray that they do not get called back. Yet, I always enjoyed the opportunity to track down these esoteric sounds, because I like mysteries.

The biggest mistake piano technicians make is to do all the tricks they know without first attempting to determine where the noise is coming from. It is as if they want to fix everything in the hope that they will stumble upon the solution. When diagnosing a strange piano noise, first attempt to find the cause. Make every effort to pinpoint the location of the noise with a little detective work. Even though this may take more time initially, it will save time and effort in the long-run. I usually identify what the noise is not, and narrow it down to what it might be. Then, I do one fix at a time. If that fix

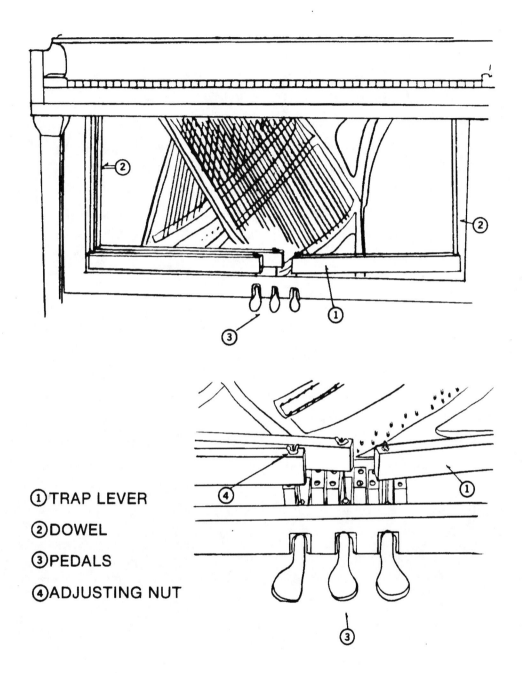

① TRAP LEVER

② DOWEL

③ PEDALS

④ ADJUSTING NUT

#20 *Vertical Piano Trapwork*

does not work, I eliminate other causes and try another. Nonetheless, all the fixes in the world will not work unless you identify the cause. I learned to identify the cause first before launching into complicated repairs the hard way. The most difficult piano noise I ever heard taught me this valuable lesson.

In Phoenix, Arizona, I tuned a Steinway model B (6'10 ½ ") grand for a professional pianist. He was a piano teacher. He practiced in the morning and taught students in the afternoon. I tuned the piano first thing in the morning. In Arizona, the mornings in May can be quite cool. Yet, the days heat up into the mid-90s and sometimes push 100 degrees. He played the piano right after the tuning and liked the results. Yet, a few days later he called me complaining that his piano had gone "horribly out of tune" during the hot afternoon and his students were complaining bitterly. Strangely, he played it in the next morning and it sounded fine. Yet each afternoon during the student lessons, it again went "wildly" out of tune. Obviously, he was greatly concerned that something was terribly wrong.

I made an appointment to investigate the cause of the piano's instability in the afternoon when the temperature was warm. Knowing that climate is a major reason pianos go out of tune, I thought that the temperature change had somehow knocked it out. The piano had a damp-chaser system installed, so it should have been very stable. Yet, when I arrived and played a few chords, I heard the strangest sounds coming from it—tinny rattles and zinging wildness in each note as if it were possessed. Not only had it gone out of tune, it sounded as if the plate had snapped and all the screws were loose in the piano. In a panic, I went right to work. I tightened all the case screws, I cinched the pedal bolts, checked for loose backcheck wires, tightened the keystop rail nuts, adjusted the grand dampers, put cotton balls into the strike plate (piano lock plate), leveled and seated the strings, replaced agraffes (the place where the string goes through before the tuning pins) that might have been too loose, reshaped and needled the hot spots on the hammers. I spent hours doing every trick I knew, yet at the end of the day, the rattles and zingings and crazy wooshing sounds were still their, and even worse than when I started! I had used every trick in my repertoire, and still had not solved the problem.

Exhausted, I gazed up at the large slowing rotating ceiling fan directly above me. I took a breath of the cool air washing over my sweaty and sore body and I wondered what I was going to do now. My eyes followed the ceiling fan turning round and round as I pondered the question. Somewhere deep in my tiredness, the answer came. I was looking right at it! Almost in answer to my question, for some unknown reason, I robotically got up and turned the fan off. When the fan's large blades completely stopped, I played the piano. It sounded fine. Apparently, the sound of the piano was bouncing off the rotating fan's blades creating bizarre zings and buzzes that sounded as if they came from inside the instrument. I had spent the better part of the day trying to fix something in the piano that didn't exist. When the afternoon got hot, my client turned on the ceiling fan, and that was when the trouble started. Thus, the mystery was solved.

This incident was the first time I encountered this particular problem. Having come from the East coast where ceiling fans were not commonplace, I did not think about the sound being a trick of the senses. I was absolutely convinced, as were he and his students, that these wild noises came directly from the instrument. Many times since then I have heard odd sounds that the owner swore came from their piano, only to find that it was a trick from the ceiling fan. Those of you with pianos in warm climates and active ceiling fans, try turning off the fan first if you hear disturbing and unusual sounds from your piano. Obviously, this was a hard lesson for me to learn.

Since then, I check the piano's immediate environment first. If I hear a strange buzz, for example, I check the picture frames and immobilize the glass in the frame. Then, I try the notes again. If the noise is still present, I look at the lamps around, near, and on the piano. Sometimes I will tighten a loose lamp nut or adjust a lampshade. I look for music lights on the music rack and adjust any loose bolts or wobbly parts. After checking the environment, then I start on the piano by tightening all the hardware screws and work my way inside.

Here are some general areas to look in the piano when troubleshooting some of the most common piano noises.

- Clicks—loose glue joints, loose hammer rest rail, loose key pins, worn key bushings, dehumidifier elements not secure, loose backchecks, loose keystop screws and nuts, loose damper stop rail, loose key top material (ivory or plastic), loose center pins

- Squeaks and Groans—damper and hammer springs, worn damper guide rail bushings, repetition spring rubbing in dirty or unlubricated repetition lever slots (especially in Steinway grand pianos), grand action return springs, unlubricated grand keybed, loose legs or pedal rods and lyre, pianos with a polyester finish squeak when they are rubbed together (the most common area is the cheek blocks), upright action rails (primarily when the sustain pedal is engaged), upright hammer rest rail

- Rattles and Buzzes—old hardened damper felt, cracked soundboard or rib, defective bass strings, de-humidifier element, locks and locking plates

- Knocks—keyframe unbedded, loose key leads, loose legs or lyre, sustenuto rod out of position

- Whooshes and Scratches—grand dampers, hammers or felts rubbing against neighbor, wood sliver catching a moving part

- Zings—strings (treble and bass), agraffes

6

PROTECTING YOUR INVESTMENT

HUMIDIFIER / DEHUMIDIFIER

Climate can have serious effects on pianos. If a piano is moved from a wet climate to a dry climate, the wood and other parts will start to split and fall apart. It may be impossible to control the climate outside the piano, but if you need to, it is possible to control the climate inside the piano with a climate control system. I recommend a climate control system only if your piano is in an area with temperature and humidity extremes. For example, if the piano is near the beach or in the desert, a climate control device is advisable. In a wet environment such as beachfront property, moist air will rust the steel parts in the piano and warp the wood in a short time. To evaporate moisture within the piano, a heater bar (dehumidifier) can be effective. It can be purchased from your piano technician or from a piano store. The heater bar is placed inside a vertical piano or underneath a grand piano. Yet there are other solutions.

One of my clients has a console piano in her beach house. Harsh, moist salt air attacks pianos kept in beach homes within a short time and I always expect to find broken strings and similar rust related problems when I service these instruments. However, from the first day I serviced this client's piano I noticed there was no rust damage, no broken strings, and no heater bar. I examined the piano carefully and found that in spite of years of being on the beach, the piano's strings were as shiny as the day the piano was bought. Her secret was a little bag of white flour that she hung inside the piano and changed every few months. Judging from what I've seen, this practice is a good, practical way to keep a vertical piano moisture free.

On the other hand, in a dry environment, a humidifier (a small reservoir with a heater bar and pads in it) should be placed inside a vertical piano or attached underneath a grand piano. When the air becomes too dry, the bar heats the water inside the bucket and provides the moisture needed to protect the piano. A humidifier can also be purchased from your piano technician or from a piano store.

If you live in an area of drastic climate changes, from humid to dry, I recommend a complete climate control system. It consists of a humidifier, dehumidifier, and humidistat control. The climate control system is self-regulating; it uses household current as its source of electrical power. A system like this gives your piano the ultimate in climate protection and works effectively and reliably for years.

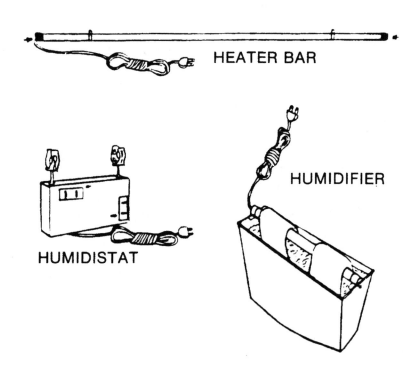

HEATER BAR

HUMIDISTAT

HUMIDIFIER

#21 *Piano Climate Control System*

MOTH PROTECTION

Moths are a common problem in pianos. They lay their eggs in dust that accumulates in piano hammers and bushings, which are made of felt. When the moth eggs hatch, the larvae eat the felt. The best moth protection is to keep your piano clean. Cleaning is essential in order to protect pianos from damage. I recommend a piano cleaning every few years. However, if you already have moths, you can do a few things to eliminate the pests.

There is a spray for demothing a piano, specifically made for piano felts, which can be purchased at a piano supply store or from your technician. Apply the spray directly to the action and hammers. As a temporary treatment to demoth a piano, mothballs can be used. Once you have demothed your piano, keep it clean and you will keep it moth-free.

WHERE TO PLACE THE PIANO IN THE HOME

Piano placement is a concern of most piano owners. You should observe a few basic rules when deciding where to place your piano in your home. Do not place the piano near a window or against an outside wall. Either of these sites provides too little protection from sunlight and climate changes. Direct sunlight will fade, peel, and checker the delicate piano finish. It is also not advisable to place the piano near a radiator, stove, or steam pipes. The heat will ruin the piano in winter months by drying out the glue used in the case and action. Do not place the piano on a concrete floor or near a cinderblock wall because these retain dampness. Pianos are sensitive to their environments. A little thought to its location will help to protect your piano for years to come.

For grand pianos, in addition to thoughtful location, it is also good planning to have a table of some kind near. It is a temptation to put drinks, candles, lamps, or breakable china on the flat surfaces on either side of the music desk. But you should be aware that the music desk is not a sturdy surface. When each note is played the music desk vibrates ever so slightly, but just enough to move most objects gradually off its surface. Many restaurant pianos are needlessly ruined by spilled drinks that were placed beside the music desk and on the lid. Inevitably, the drink falls onto the pins, piano action, damper felts, soundboard, and other delicate parts gumming up the action. One restaurant piano had all of its felts eaten by ants after a sugary drink spilled off the music desk into the action. Needless to say, repairing major damage like this was costly. A good way to avoid the temptation to place objects on the music desk is to have a coffee table beside the piano for drinks, lamps, pictures, etc. The piano is a wonderful piece of furniture and a vibrant, alive, musical instrument that is not designed to support anything other than sheet music.

A PIANO'S WORTH

On the Southern Californian coast in the mid 1970s, the piano market was full of late nineteenth century vertical pianos that had been shipped from England. Built in extraordinarily beautiful cases of ornately crafted fine wood with attached candelabras, these pianos were about one hundred years old when they arrived. These old English pianos, with so-called "bird-cage" actions, have internal parts of different sizes from those of pianos built today. This makes their part replacement difficult and their servicing financially impractical. Tuning pianos with bird cage actions is a complicated chore requiring far more time and effort than a tuner can give without charging a substantial amount of money. He must remove the dampers to tune this style piano, which means that the notes won't stop ringing when played. Therefore he is forced to chip" or pluck the strings when tuning.

Many tuners and technicians refused to service these instruments, and the pianos quickly went from piano stores to antique stores for sale to the general public. Unfortunately, a number of people looking for bargains purchased these old pianos. Many of them unknowingly bought a nice piece of furniture that was totally useless as a musical instrument. One such person called me to service his old English piano. We came to the conclusion that it would be far less expensive for him to rent a piano for his daughter's lessons than to try to rebuild the piano he owned. At least his daughter would have a quality instrument to play and one that would be much cheaper to maintain.

When judging a piano's worth, look at the inside as well as the outside of the case. See whether the tuning pins are tight and whether the hammers look good, and check to be sure that all of the notes function properly. Remember that a piano is valued by appearance and function. It is truly unfortunate when unsuspecting parents buy a piano for their children to learn on and the piano has one problem after another. Constantly needed repairs destroy the child's will to learn and drain the parents' pocketbook. It is better to buy a quality instrument for your initial investment and enjoy years of trouble-free music than to buy a "bargain" and suffer years of dissatisfaction.

In the last analysis, the piano player is the one who should make the final decision on what piano to purchase. Two pianos can be built by the same piano manufacturer, on the same day, with the same style and materials, and look exactly alike, but sound completely different because each one is unique. Pianos can differ subtly, and yet profoundly. This is the nature of the instrument. Piano purchasing is a highly personal venture because what appeals to one individual may not appeal to another. So listen and be sure.

Now that you know more about pianos and how they function, don't be afraid to look at the action and the strings; pay careful attention to the tone, and decide exactly what you want. In this way, you will become a more educated consumer, and you will be happy with your rather expensive purchase. It could be your one piano purchase for a lifetime.

If you have your piano tuned and checked regularly before problems develop, its value will increase as the years go by. A properly tuned and maintained piano can be a source of great joy and many hours of fulfillment. The piano is a combination of steel, wood, iron, brass, plastic, and felt forming one of the most beautiful and sensitive instruments ever conceived.

Enjoy your piano, discover its true value, and protect it from the environment. It cost a substantial amount of money to acquire a piano in the first place. It makes good sense to do everything you can to preserve your investment.

Many old upright pianos survived generations in the same family, in the same house, and often in the same room, only to deteriorate majestically. The piano was never used. Life passed it by until finally a decision was made to junk the old beast. Eventually, the piano was hauled away to the closest dump where it was shattered into little pieces, never to be seen again. All too often, this sad end to an old upright was a normal occurrence, resulting in more pianos ending up at the dump than were being rebuilt.

Today things are different. People are learning that the old upright pianos have a sound and tone quality not easily found in newer, smaller instruments. One of the things our family did when we were all active in the piano business was to look for fine pianos and bring them into our shop for rebuilding or reconditioning. We usually had several around, awaiting a facelift. One was a beautiful quarter-grained oak piano, not quite as tall as the tallest upright. This piano received special attention. Upon completion, it sold immediately, and there were several potential buyers who were disappointed at missing the opportunity to purchase this fine instrument.

At the same time, over in the corner of the shop was a large, horribly painted piano, which always seemed to be in the way and was always being moved to make room for some other piano. It was an ex-player piano without the player mechanism, and with intricately carved designs in the wood. The legs were extensively carved. Anyone who knows about furniture refinishing recognizes how hard it is to remove paint from carved wood. The fact remained that, before a new finish could be put on, the old one had to come off. Finally, just to get it out of the shop, we began work on this piano.

Indeed, refinishing it was no small job, yet it was rewarding. To our great delight, under the ugly paint was beautiful mahogany wood that had appealing markings and refinished beautifully with clear varnish. Next, the inside of the piano was completely reconditioned. Work there was just as rewarding. The resulting tone was rich and beautiful, comparable to that of a good-sized grand piano. If there is an old upright piano in your family, maybe it isn't really an old beast. Who knows?

Some things turn out well, but sometimes results are less than satisfying. In the early days, when my father was just becoming known for rebuilding and reconditioning pianos, he answered an ad for a grand piano that someone wanted to sell. It was in a barn and had the remnants of a player mechanism in it. Mice, squirrels, and other rodents had made their homes in the player action and throughout the piano; their little skeletons were everywhere. The odor of dead things and animal waste was overwhelming. However, the owner wanted us to haul it away and the piano was taken to our shop. Everything inside the piano was so dirty and smelly that we just removed the player mechanism and hauled it off to the dump.

Several months later, while talking to a piano technician who repairs and restores player pianos, my father learned that the old player was, in fact, a vintage *reproducer*. A reproducer not only strikes the notes, as any player does, but provides shading in tone as well. A reproducer is to a regular player piano as a Rembrandt is to a paint by-numbers kit. It is said that once a reproducing grand was played behind a screen at Carnegie Hall and that the audience thought for certain that a person was playing. We had thrown away thousands of dollars in irreplaceable reproducer mechanisms. Live and learn. We felt bad, it's true, but the real loser in this story was the original owner, who had no idea of the value of the instrument rotting away in his barn.

By following the recommendations for the care and maintenance of your piano, you will safeguard your investment as much as is humanly possible. Yet you may have to place a piano in a detrimental location because you have no space along an inside wall in your home. Or perhaps your family spends part of the year in one house and part in another, leaving the piano, or two pianos if there is one at each location, alone and unattended for an extended period of time. Necessity may dictate unfavorable conditions for a piano, but the desire to have a piano at all is sometimes overriding, even when it is known that proper care cannot be given to it. In a situation like this, it must be understood that the piano will be subjected to factors of environment that will affect it adversely. It is amazing, nevertheless, how well a piano can withstand unfavorable treatment and conditions without being relegated to uselessness. So do the best you can as far as protection is concerned. Whatever the circumstances, the most important thing you can do is to use and enjoy your piano. Allow this beautiful creation to enrich your life.

GLOSSARY

BALANCE PIN—pin located in the center of the piano key, also called balance rail pin

BOTTOM BOARD—supports the trapwork on the bottom of a vertical piano

BRIDGE—long, irregular shaped piece of wood attached to the soundboard that keeps the strings in proper position and helps to transmit string vibrations

BRIDLE STRAP—cloth tape that aids in the hammer's return on vertical pianos

CLIMATE CONTROL SYSTEM—dehumidifier, humidifier, and humidistat designed to ensure the proper humidity within the piano

CONSOLE PIANO—vertical piano forty to forty-nine inches tall with the piano action located directly on top of the piano keys, sometimes referred to as the studio upright

CROWN—gradual curvature of the soundboard

DAMPER—piece of felt that allows the note to vibrate when lifted off the string

DOWELS—parts of the trapwork that connect the trap levers to the vertical piano's action

DROP ACTION—term used for the spinet piano action located below the piano keys

DROP STICKER—spinet piano part that connects the piano key to lifter elbow, also called lifter wires

EASING PLIERS—pliers specifically designed to squeeze piano key bushings

ESCAPEMENT—general term for the action parts that aid in hammer return

FALLBOARD—that part of the piano case that covers and protects the piano keys when the piano is not in use

FALL STRIP—a long narrow piece of wood extending the length of the piano, located between the piano keys and the fallboard, also called drop rail

FRONT RAIL PIN—pin located under the playing surface of the piano key

GRAND PIANO—piano with strings in a horizontal position

HAMMER—that part of the piano action assembly made of felt, glued and tacked to a wood molding, which strikes the string when a note is played

HAMMER BUTT—base onto which vertical piano hammers are attached

JACK—L-shaped part of a piano's action that pushes the hammer toward the string when a note is played

JACK SPRING—spring attached to the base of the jack to aid in the hammer's return after a note is sounded

KEY BED—frame onto which the piano keys and action are mounted

KEYBLOCK—rectangular block of wood located at each end of the keyboard

KEYBOARD—the piano's keys

KEY BUSHING—felt padding discreetly glued to the piano key, protects the key from front rail pin and balance pin abrasion

KEYS—solid pieces of soft wood whose striking surfaces are covered with plastic or ivory

LID—moveable top cover of the piano case

LIFTER ELBOW—connects drop stickers (lifter wires) to the wippen in spinet pianos

LOWER FRAME—visible board forming the bottom face of a vertical piano case

LYRE—supports the pedals on a grand piano

MUSIC DESK—area above the keyboard for holding music

MUSIC SHELF—the part of a vertical piano case that supports the music desk

PIANO ACTION—piano mechanism that transfers the striking force from the keys to the strings when a note is played

PIANO CASE—exterior body of the piano, also called the piano frame

PINBLOCK—laminated hardwood block attached

underneath the plate to hold the tuning pins in position

PLATE—also called harp, made of cast iron and serves as the primary support for the strings

PRACTICE PEDAL—center pedal on vertical pianos, when held down, it positions a thick felt strip between the hammers and the strings which reduces the piano's volume significantly

SEASONAL PITCH CHANGE—piano's general pitch variance; higher in spring and lower in winter

SOFT PEDAL—left pedal on grand and vertical pianos

grand piano—shifts entire action a little to the right causing the treble hammers to strike only two strings per note, also called the una corda pedal

vertical piano—moves all the hammers closer to the strings, reducing hammer travel and force when striking the strings

SOSTENUTO PEDAL—center pedal on most grand and vertical pianos

grand piano - sustains the notes that are played just before and while the pedal is depressed

vertical piano - sustains all the bass notes when depressed

SOUNDBOARD—large board that forms the back of a vertical piano or the bottom of a grand piano; (it) vibrates when the notes are played and amplifies the sound of the strings

SOUNDBOARD STEEL—flat piece of spring steel with a hole in one end, used in cleaning grand piano soundboards

SPINET PIANO—smallest of the vertical pianos, less than forty inches tall, has the action located below key level

SPINET REPLACEMENT ELBOW—plastic or wood lifter elbow designed for easy replacement on spinet pianos

STICKERS—part of the upright piano action that rests on the piano keys and attaches to the action

STRINGS—piano wire which is wrapped around a tuning pin and held by the plate, which produces sound when struck by the hammers; also called music wire

SUPPORT BLOCK—supports the action in a spinet piano

SUSTAINING PEDAL—the right-most pedal on grand and vertical pianos, raises all of the dampers off the strings when held down; also called the loud pedal

TRAP LEVERS—those parts of a vertical piano trapwork that connect the pedals to the dowels

TRAPWORK—general term for the complete pedal assembly

TUNING PINS—threaded steel pins driven into the pinblock which maintain the strings' tension

TUNING PIN SETTER—tool designed to hold the tuning pin in place while the pin is hammered deeper into the pinblock; used to remedy loose or slipping tuning pins

UNICHORD PIANO—piano with one string for each note

UPRIGHT PIANO—tallest of the vertical pianos, fifty inches or more, has the piano action located above the keys

VERTICAL PIANO—piano with strings in a vertical position

VOICING—manipulating a piano's hammers to enhance its tone

WIPPEN—the part of a piano action that transfers the striking force from the key to the hammer

NOTES

NOTES

NOTES